Praise for *Make Your Move*

"*Make Your Move* is perfect and perfectly timed for me, personally. I used to think I was an assertive dater, but not compared to the smart women whose stories Jon Birger tells in his new book. I will now go forth bolder than ever! With data and real-life examples of women who have taken command of their dating lives, *Make Your Move* will give you the skills and the confidence you need to win at love."

—Ylonda Gault, author of *Child, Please: How Mama's Old-School Lessons Helped Me Check Myself Before I Wrecked Myself*

"Rules are meant to be broken and dating culture has been long overdue for a rewrite. As a dating coach of 15+ years, I have always recommended that female clients take control of their love lives and witnessed how that consistently leads to more matches than a chivalry-led strategy. *Make Your Move* expertly outlines this argument and gives women the tools to find quality partners in this changing dating landscape."

—Damona Hoffman, advice columnist for the *LA Times* and host of *The Dates & Mates* Podcast

"Every day my patients tell me about failed relationships and dating disasters. The majority of women who freeze their eggs are doing it because they have not found the right partner. Jon Birger's new book explains why traditional dating advice fails so many of these women—pushing them to play games or conceal career goals just to land a man. I highly recommend *Make Your Move* to women who are frustrated with the state of modern dating."

—Dr. Lynn Westphal, chief medical officer of Kindbody and former director of Stanford University's Fertility Preservation Program

"*Make Your Move* is a book that provides clarity during a confusing time for singles. Dating's old "rules" don't work anymore. Today's new era demands a new guidebook for how to seek and create lasting relationships. Thankfully we have Jon Birger, who weaves analytical research, exhaustive reporting, and fun storytelling into practical counsel that moves past all the outdated thinking and tired advice on dating. *Make Your Move*, in a way no other work has, helps us rethink who we want and how to meet them."

—Sridhar Pappu "The Male Animal" columnist

MAKE YOUR MOVE

Also by Jon Birger

Date-onomics (2015)

MAKE YOUR MOVE

The New Science of Dating and Why Women Are in Charge

JON BIRGER

BenBella Books, Inc.
Dallas, Texas

BenBella Books, Inc.
10440 N. Central Expressway
Suite 800
Dallas, TX 75231
www.benbellabooks.com
Send feedback to feedback@benbellabooks.com

BenBella is a federally registered trademark.

Printed in the United States of America
10 9 8 7 6 5 4 3 2 1

Library of Congress Control Number: 2020034733
ISBN 978-1-948836-90-6 (trade paper)
ISBN 978-1-950665-62-4 (ebook)

Copyediting by Jennifer Greenstein
Proofreading by Jenny Bridges and Cape Cod Compositors, Inc.
Text design by PerfecType, Nashville, TN
Cover design by Kerry Rubenstein
Printed by Lake Book Manufacturing

Distributed to the trade by Two Rivers Distribution, an Ingram brand
www.tworiversdistribution.com

Special discounts for bulk sales are available. Please contact
bulkorders@benbellabooks.com.

CONTENTS

The stories and conversations in this book are true and based on my interviews with individuals or re-created from my memories of them. Interviewees identified only by first names have been given aliases. Some biographical details have been altered to protect their privacy.

PREFACE: FIRST,
A LITTLE BACKSTORY

My friend Samantha spotted me as I was leaving the gym. "Hey, big guy, wait up!"

A fifty-four-year-old travel agent, Sam had just finished reading my first book, *Date-onomics*, and I could tell she was itching to give me her review.

Writers are an insecure lot. Personally, I'd rather wait in line at the Department of Motor Vehicles for two hours than listen to Sam, or any other friend, critique one of my books. While I love Sam to death—she and I have been workout buddies for years—she also happens to be one of those people who are never shy about giving uncensored, unfiltered opinions about anything. So this was not exactly a conversation I was looking forward to.

Date-onomics explored how today's increasingly lopsided sex ratios among college graduates have given rise to hookup culture and declining marriage rates. Since 2000, four women have graduated from college for every three men. As a result, there are now 10.3 million women versus 8.1 million men among US college graduates under age thirty-five. So, no, it's not all in your head. There really aren't enough marriageable men.

Of course, this man deficit—a shortage of college-educated men, to be precise—would not matter if we were all more open-minded about whom we date and marry. Problem is, at the same time college enrollments have been skewing female, there's been a simultaneous rise in what academics call "assortative mating." That's a fancy way of saying college graduates increasingly want to marry only other grads.

My own belief was, and is, that white-collar women and blue-collar men will eventually get sick of being toyed with by the opposite sex. Eventually they'll find each other, creating a boom in what I dubbed "mixed-collar" dating. But until this happens—until people finally realize that a college degree does not make someone a better wife or a better husband—the college gender gap will continue to make dating difficult and sometimes heartbreaking for college-educated women.

The problem goes beyond mere statistics. My core argument in *Date-onomics* was that the emergence of modern hookup culture has little to do with Tinder or porn or Facebook—or anything else modern scolds like to blame—and everything to do with today's lopsided sex ratios among college grads. The dating scene becomes more sexualized and less monogamous when women are in oversupply. Hetero men are in less of a rush to settle down, and women start playing by different rules too.

No, I don't think singles are doing a head count and then making a conscious decision to behave differently. It's more of a "When in Rome, do as the Romans do" phenomenon—one that seems to be hardwired into human biology. When males are plentiful, the mating culture tends to be more monogamous; when males are scarce, it's less so. (Same-sex dating is largely unaffected by sex ratios. Gay men don't care how many or how few women there are, just as queer women don't care how many or how few men there are.)

Of course, what's apocalyptic for some women can be perfectly palatable for others. A few years ago, a thirtysomething woman in an open relationship nearly bit my head off when I suggested during a book talk that lopsided sex ratios were contributing to the rising popularity of polyamory (also known as consensual non-monogamy). Lots of young men and women embrace this lifestyle, and, as I learned the hard way, they resent any suggestion that their interest is influenced by anything other than merit or personal preference. According to one survey, 17 percent of Americans ages eighteen to twenty-nine now report having had sex outside their relationship with the consent of their partners. That compares to just 9 percent for those ages forty-five to sixty-four.[1]

I'm not passing judgment. Consensual non-monogamy is a valid lifestyle choice, as is traditional marriage, as is staying single. The point I've always emphasized is that demographics and culture are intertwined. We saw this in the 1920s when the shortage of young men in the West gave rise to the Flapper Generation and the loosening sexual mores of the Roaring Twenties. Ten million soldiers died in World War I and twenty million more were wounded, many grievously. The consequences were captured eloquently by author Irène Némirovsky in her novel *The Fires of Autumn*, set in 1920s France. Némirovsky tells the story of a young war widow named Thérèse who thinks she is being courted for marriage by her childhood friend Bernard, only to discover that Bernard wants nothing more than a fling.

Bernard is baffled by Thérèse's unwillingness to carry on a casual affair. Given the dearth of young men in postwar Europe, Bernard wonders why any bachelor would ever choose to settle down. "You want to have some fun? Fine," he tells Thérèse. "You don't? Goodbye. There are too many women and they're all too easy to make it worthwhile."[2]

Demographics and culture converged again in the 1960s and '70s, leading to another time of sexual liberation. Back then, women preferred to marry men three or four years their senior. Birth rates rose sharply during the 1945–1965 Baby Boom. Fast-forward twenty years, and suddenly there weren't enough men born in 1944 for all the women born in 1948. Writing in the 1970s, Harvard University psychologist Marcia Guttentag argued that lopsided sex ratios among Baby Boomer men and women were the driving force behind the sexual revolution of her era. Whenever women are in oversupply, Guttentag wrote, "constraints on sexuality fade [and] promiscuity increases . . . Women are more likely than men to have experienced abandonment, desertion, or betrayal; they are more likely to develop a feeling of having been exploited."[3] Guttentag went on to posit that the rise of the feminist movement in her era was essentially a backlash against the misogynistic culture created by lopsided sex ratios—one in which women were increasingly objectified and devalued. Were Guttentag alive today, I suspect she'd be drawing similar connections between the college gender gap and the subsequent rise of the #MeToo movement.

I interviewed dozens of single, college-educated women for *Date-onomics*, most of them distraught or exasperated by their inability to find suitable partners. My interviewees were generally engaging and attractive, with successful careers as doctors, television reporters, advertising executives, and the like. These women had everything going for them, yet they couldn't seem to find a decent guy who wouldn't bail the moment things got serious. As successful as these women were professionally, romantically they felt like failures.

I interviewed married women for *Date-onomics* too, and they were just thankful to be off the dating treadmill. One happily married woman I interviewed was shaking visibly while recounting her single years in New York City, before she met her husband. She shared story after story of being misled by men whom she thought she might marry.

"I didn't understand what I was doing wrong," she confided. "Those were the worst years of my life."

My friend Sam told me that she was moved by these women's stories. They really resonated with her, she said. And I was incredibly relieved to hear this—until, that is, Sam started to explain exactly why their stories resonated. It was *not* because Sam could relate to these women personally. Sam herself hadn't experienced any of these problems. It was simply because the women of *Date-onomics* sounded exactly like her own single friends.

"You could have been writing about half the women I know," Sam told me, our conversation spilling out into the gym parking lot. "They have this damsels-in-distress, woe-is-me attitude, always complaining that nobody ever asks them out."

Sam wasn't saying this to be cruel. The women she was talking about were her friends. She sounded less like a scold and more like a frustrated parent trying to teach a willful five-year-old how to tie his shoes properly.

I didn't like where this conversation was headed.

"You know," she continued, "you really should have talked to me first. I could have helped these women."

I started to feel sick.

Truth is, I *had* thought about interviewing Sam for *Date-onomics*. I should have interviewed her. The only reason I didn't is because I knew enough about Sam's personal life to know it wouldn't fit my narrative. Married twice and proposed to seven times, Sam has never, ever, had the least bit of trouble finding long-term relationships with the men of her choice. Mind you, Sam's love life has not been perfect, and she would be the first to admit this. She wishes that she had worked harder to save her first marriage, for instance. (Her first husband was an airline executive who traveled frequently for work, and they grew apart during his absences.) What's important about Sam's life story, though—and what probably dissuaded me from interviewing her in the first place—is that whatever romantic disappointments she has experienced over her life, they were never for lack of options. Sam has lived all over—Colorado, Japan, California, New York. Wherever she's lived, finding relationships with men she likes has never been a problem.

Before Sam and I spoke at the gym that morning, I honestly didn't know why Sam's experiences were so different from those of other women. I figured it was a fluke. I thought maybe she was some sort of outlier. But the longer Sam and I spoke, the more foolish I felt for not having interviewed her. If I had, Sam could have helped me solve what turned out to be *Date-onomics*'s biggest shortcoming.

———

Date-onomics was more pop science than a traditional self-help book. My editor kept pressing me for more dating advice, but the best I could offer were small ways for women to improve their dating odds—such as moving to cities where sex ratios were more balanced. I didn't have that one big, bold, new dating strategy that could help all my readers beat the odds in a dating market so stacked against young women.

But Sam did have such a strategy.

Sam's knack for landing the men of her choice was not a fluke. She was not lucky at love. Nor was she good at dating simply because she's fit and attractive. So too were many of the women I interviewed for *Date-onomics*.

No, the reason Sam has always succeeded where other women fail is because she has spent her entire life ignoring all the conventional warnings and wisdom passed along to young women by generations of moms, sisters, and married friends—and reinforced by a cottage industry of dating books, from *The Rules* to *Ignore the Guy, Get the Guy.*

As Sam explained to me, "The women in your book sound like badasses. They need to date like badasses too."

What did Sam mean by this?

She meant having the confidence to make the first move with men of your choice. No more sitting back and hoping the guy you like notices you. Badass women don't wait for their phones to ring or their dating apps to ding. They don't settle for the options presented to them. They go after whomever and whatever they want.

> "The women in your book sound like badasses. They need to date like badasses too."

"Ah, it's the feminist approach to dating," I replied. (I'm always thinking of titles for my next book project!)

Sam grimaced.

"Honestly, I don't think of myself as a big feminist. I'm more of a romantic. The important thing is I decide for myself who I like and who I'm attracted to. Why should we leave it all up to the men?"

And that, Sam told me, is precisely what she would have told the lonely women of *Date-onomics*—if only I'd asked her. It's what she's been telling her own friends for years.

"I'll give you an example," Sam said. "I was out at a bar with my friend Lisa, who was the classic damsel in distress. Very pretty but always complaining that nobody asks her out. 'Am I fat?' . . . 'Am I ugly?' . . . 'Why don't men find me attractive?' . . . And on and on.

"I kept telling her, 'You have to get out of that mindset. Maybe there's something about you that the men are nervous about. Maybe they don't think you're approachable.'

"Anyway, one night we're at a bar in Connecticut and there was a man standing behind her who she seemed to like. They were talking a little bit, he wasn't wearing a ring, and when he stepped away for a second, I kicked her and said, 'Just ask him out. You may never see him again.'"

Lisa didn't want to. She was scared. But Sam wouldn't let her off the hook.

"When he got back, Lisa turned around and asked him if he'd like to have dinner sometime. Well, nine months later he proposed. A year after that they were married."

Sam's whole life has been this type of master class in making the first move. She made the first move with all but one of her long-term relationships (more on *that* guy later). She even made the first move with boys back in high school, which always drew furious rebukes from the queen bees at her high school. The worst came after she walked up to the star of the basketball team and invited him to go to junior prom with her.

"They were just mad that he said yes!" Sam recalled with a devil-may-care grin. "But boy did I catch a lot of shit. There was a lot of 'There goes that daughter-of-a-whore Riley girl again'"—a slut-shamey reference to the fact that Sam's mom, a widow, had a live-in boyfriend.

Sam's willingness to flip the script on dating's traditional gender roles has a lot to do with how she was raised. A military brat who moved five times before turning eighteen, Sam learned early on that she wouldn't have any friends at all if she just sat back and waited for others to befriend her. For Sam, being reserved or coy was a surefire path to loneliness.

Another thing Sam had going for her was a strong role model in her mother, Betty. Your parents' relationship often influences your own love life, and that was certainly true for Sam.

I asked her how her mom and dad first met. "Mom always wanted to marry a sailor," Sam replied.

Betty had been a young, single woman living in Southern California, and one day she played hooky from work in order to greet the US Navy fleet as it arrived home from the Korean War. Before long she was locking eyes with a handsome sailor with a warm smile and nobody there to greet him.

She walked up and introduced herself.

"Would you like to go get a coffee?" Betty asked him.

The answer from the young sailor was a very enthusiastic "Yes."

The rest, as they say, is history. Betty and the sailor—Sam's dad—were married two weeks later.

"My dad passed away too young, but they had a happy life together. Mom always said to me, 'Sam, your dad and I had twenty-two great years together. If you see something you want, step in and go after it.'"

Sam's assertive streak didn't always endear her to other women, but men always seemed to appreciate it.

"Men love it when a confident woman is attracted to them," said Sam.

For Sam, the biggest benefit to making the first move is it gives her so many more men to choose from. Tall, blonde, and athletic, Sam is blessed with good looks that have always been catnip to the wrong guys and intimidating to the ones she liked. Making the first move allows her to date the men whom *she* prefers, not just those with the nerve to approach her.

"I don't trust guys who have no fear of rejection. They're too superficial. They're the ones just looking for a good time," Sam told me. "The men other women hope will ask them out, they're usually the ones I try to avoid."

After college, Sam moved to San Francisco and took a job in marketing with a major airline. A friend at work knew a guy in another department whom she thought Sam would like. Sam and her friend then hatched a plan for Sam to meet the young executive, Paul, at a company picnic.

The plan worked. Sam and Paul chatted over hot dogs, and by the end of the day, they were on opposing teams in the finals of the company volleyball tournament.

"I was twenty-four, and he was twenty-nine and coming off a really bad divorce," Sam said of Paul, the man who would become her first husband.

"One of the things I instantly liked about him is that he was nice to the women on his team. He passed the ball to them, which a lot of the other guys wouldn't do," Sam recalled. "He was kind but also so, so shy. It was clear his confidence was shot after the divorce."

Sam knew she would have to make the first move with Paul. "So I made a little bet with him. I said that if my team won, he'd have to take me out for dinner. And if his team won, I'd buy him dinner. And before we left, I made sure we agreed on the date, time, and restaurant."

> "He told me he never would have made the first move if I hadn't. He didn't think someone like me would be attracted to him."

Two years later Sam and Paul were married, and that volleyball game became their meet-cute.

"We used to talk about it a lot," said Sam. "He told me he never would have made the first move if I hadn't. He didn't think someone like me would be attracted to him.

"He didn't want to get embarrassed or turned down. His first wife had left him, and he was sort of broken by that. I took away all the tension for him. There wasn't any thought of, 'Oh my gosh, does she like me?' He knew I liked him."

Sam's friends were shocked by her bravado.

"Their reaction was basically, 'How did you have the nerve? Weren't you afraid he'd turn you down? You hardly knew him—what if it turned out he was crazy?'

"All I knew is that I was really attracted to him and he seemed like a really good person. I felt it was worth taking the risk."

As I said, Sam and Paul's story did not have the fairy-tale ending—they divorced after sixteen years of marriage. But they did raise two terrific children together, and they remain friends.

The same cannot be said for Sam's only serious relationship in which the man made the first move.

Sam moved to New York City after her divorce from Paul. On a lark, she agreed to join a coworker at a speed-dating event. A reporter from a local magazine was there and asked if she and her photographer could follow Sam around from table to table and document her experience. Sam agreed.

Dating-wise, the event was a bit of a bust. Sam was in her forties and most of the men were twenty years her junior.

"I told one of them I was old enough to be his mom," Sam recalled.

That quip, along with a glamorous photo of Sam that ran with the article, caught the attention of Jack, a New York City hedge fund manager. Jack checked off all Wall Street stereotypes—slicked-back hair, insane confidence, and a jet-black Porsche Carrera that matched his personality. He would have fit in perfectly on the Showtime series *Billions*.

Jack told his secretary to call the magazine reporter and get Sam's phone number, which she did. Jack then phoned Sam, introduced himself, and asked her out on a date. Sam said yes, and the first date turned into a six-month relationship that was a bit of a whirlwind.

Jack wasn't exactly Sam's type, but he was handsome and wealthy and she didn't know a lot of people in New York at the time. Plus, Sam loves to travel, and dating Jack did entail spur-of-the-moment trips to the Caribbean and the Hamptons.

But the fun times ended abruptly. One evening, Jack asked Sam to join him for dinner at his country club with a few Wall

Street buddies. The dinner conversation soon turned to politics. Jack and his friends were dyed-in-the-wool Republicans, George W. Bush voters, and supporters of the war in Iraq. A lifelong liberal, Sam was on the opposite side of the political spectrum. Like I said, Sam calls 'em like she sees 'em, and that night her outspokenness led to a heated argument with Jack and his friends about the Iraq War.

"The moment we got back into the car after dinner, he started yelling at me," Sam said. "I had embarrassed him. I should have known my place. Never again was I allowed to argue with him or his friends in public.

"Well, no man is going to tell me what I can or can't say. My response was basically, 'Fuck you.' It was the last time I saw him."

For Sam, the experience confirmed what she already knew: Dating is easier when she does the choosing. "After that, I swore to myself that I'd never again get into a situation where I felt I had to make it work with whichever guy was interested in me, just so I'm not lonely."

Inspired by Sam and the other women you'll meet in the pages that follow, *Make Your Move* picks up where *Date-onomics* left off—offering women bold new ideas on how to beat the odds in a dating market that's horribly unfair to educated women. Underlying it all are two core beliefs: (1) Getting different results sometimes requires a different approach, and (2) women *can* win at romance by making the first move with men.

The word *can* is italicized for good reason. *Make Your Move* shows you how to find love by flipping dating's traditional gender roles. What this book does not do is castigate single women who still prefer old-fashioned courtship. Just as a Gordon Ramsay cookbook does not force anyone to eat Beef Wellington, I would never ask any singles to do something that would make them miserable. Dating is not a one-size-fits-all endeavor. Making the first move will not be for everyone—neither is marriage, monogamy, or different-sex dating, for that matter. This book is written for women who are ready to try a radical new approach. If that's not you, no worries. But if that is you—if you are a single, hetero, marriage-minded woman who's been let down by all the conventional dating advice and conventional dating books—please keep reading.

Bear in mind that I do not have the typical résumé for a dating book author. I am not a psychologist, nor am I a matchmaker or a dating coach. I'm a journalist by trade. Indeed, the question I got all the time after writing *Date-onomics* was this: "How the heck did you—a married, fortysomething business writer best known for writing about super-boring stuff like oil and gas and the stock market—ever end up writing a book about *dating?*"

Here's the backstory. I spent ten years as a senior writer for *Money* and *Fortune*, two magazines where the editorial staffs were disproportionately female. I could not help but notice that most of the men I worked with were happily coupled whereas most of the women were unhappily single.

The discrepancy was so striking that I began to wonder why.

Why was it that so many of my female friends had these awful dating stories and dating histories, whereas my male friends—most of whom seemed to have far less going for them dating-wise (sorry, guys!)—never seemed to have any trouble at all? I wanted to unravel the mystery of why dating had become so much more difficult for women than for men.

When I first began working on *Date-onomics*, I did not think I was embarking on a new career. I thought the book would be a one-off—that I'd go back to being *Fortune's* oil and gas expert, while still penning the occasional "Five Stocks to Buy Now" column. But then *Date-onomics* was published, and everything changed. Advance copies and press releases were sent out on a Monday, and by Friday I had *Good Morning America*, *Glamour*, National Public Radio, *Time* magazine, the *Washington Post*, and a dozen other media outlets all clamoring for interviews. They thought I had cracked the code on why dating had become so impossibly hard for young, college-educated women.

But the longer my book tour lasted and the more questions I fielded from reporters and readers, the more I realized that cracking that code had been only half the job. Yes, power is knowledge. And yes, women were relieved to hear that their dating woes weren't really their fault. But the women who showed up at my book events still wanted me to tell them how to find their Mr. Rights. They wanted solutions, not just explanations. They wanted me to reveal the secrets of the women who still managed to get their guys *in spite of the lopsided dating market*. As one of my lecture-goers put it, "Why is it that the bitchy women never seem to have any problems?"

I didn't have a great answer for her then, but I do now.

Those women are not bitchy. They're bold. They're assertive. In other words, they're exactly like Sam.

> ## Join the Conversation on the
> ## *Make Your Move* Blog at JonBirger.com
>
> What's the boldest first move you've ever made with a man? How did it work out?

MAKE YOUR MOVE

1

BREAKING THE RULES

My friend Brian Howie is host and creator of a touring comedy show called *The Great Love Debate*.[1] It's part live comedy act, part town hall on the current state of dating. The show revolves around answering—or at least *trying* to answer—some all-too-familiar dating questions such as "Why is dating so hard?" and "How do we make dating easier?"

As host, Brian moderates a lighthearted discussion between a panel of local dating experts on stage (folks like me) and several hundred singles in the audience. I've been on stage for six of these shows, and a common theme involves women wishing that men were bolder. Women keep saying they want men to be more direct when it comes to expressing romantic interest and asking women out on dates. As one woman put it at my very first *Great Love Debate:* "Where the fuck did all the John Waynes go?"

Brian employs a role-playing experiment to help answer such questions. He pulls from the audience one male volunteer (a guy who claims he has game) and one female volunteer (a woman who claims she's approachable) and then tells them to pretend they're in line at Starbucks. *His* job is to pick *her* up.

Two minutes on the clock—go!

After a few minutes of either hilarity or cringe-inducing awkwardness, the audience and the panel perform a kind of postmortem on what just transpired. Three of the six times I've participated in the show, the male volunteer wound up touching the woman in order to get her attention—that is, putting his hand on her arm, her back, or her shoulder.

Brian always surveys the women in the audience for reactions, and the feedback on the touching is always the same. One-third of the women hate the touching and consider it harassment. One-third don't mind it. And one-third say they'd want the guy to touch them only if they thought the guy was cute. I mentioned this to my twenty-eight-year-old personal trainer, Victoria, after one of the shows. Her reaction: "Oh, I *totally* like it if I'm at a party and a hot guy puts his arm around me. But if he's gross looking? No way!"

Needless to say, this begs the question of how guys are supposed to know whether or not they're touch-worthy. It also offers insight into why today's single men may be less assertive than prior generations of men. If dating behavior that was once considered routine may now be taken as inappropriate, it's just not realistic to expect today's men to suddenly channel their inner John Waynes.

My friend Steve attended a *Great Love Debate* and came away with a similar reaction. What the women in the audience claimed they wanted from men did not jibe with his own experiences as a single man. A turning point for Steve was a date he went on not long after the 2018 Aziz Ansari debacle[2]—when a woman wrote an online essay about the comedy star ignoring her verbal and nonverbal cues as their first date became sexual.

"I went on a date the following week," said Steve, a forty-year-old writer who wants to meet someone nice and get married. "When I called her the next day, she told me—and this is almost verbatim—that she was uncomfortable when I tried to hold her hand and that I didn't pick up on physical cues.

"So yeah, I'm definitely much more fearful of being aggressive."

I had coffee with Brian Howie in early 2018. I wanted to find out how the Starbucks experiment was playing out in the post-#MeToo era.

"It's been a total disaster," Brian said. "Forget about touching. Most of the guys now are afraid to even say hello."

He was not exaggerating. A few months later, I was on the expert panel for one of his shows again, and the guy Brian selected for the Starbucks experiment was so nervous and tongue-tied that the whole experiment started to feel cruel and unusual.

Fear of being accused of harassment seems to have morphed into male hysteria. I'd compare it to my own mother's ongoing refusal to board an airplane nineteen years after 9/11 (never mind that flying commercial airlines has never been safer). Obviously the #MeToo movement is not a response to cheesy pickup lines or to men making clumsy passes at New Year's Eve parties. Very few women would publicly shame a guy for attempting to hold her hand. Nevertheless, the small possibility of a come-on being equated with harassment is something lots of guys don't want to deal with, even if they know deep down that their fears are overblown.

The question is not whether the post-#MeToo world is better. I think we can all agree that it is. The question is how single men and women must adapt to a dating marketplace that's been changed by #MeToo.

Said Brian, "Men used to worry about being rejected. Now they are worried about being labeled a predator."

There's so much mistrust nowadays that Brian has started to worry about his show's future, despite the fact that most *Great Love Debates* are still sold out. There's too much anger, he told me. Not enough laughter. People end up leaving more confused than when they arrived.

"Every show, we spend like twenty minutes on 'What would you like us to do, ladies?' and nobody really has a strong answer," Brian said. "There's too much yelling, and it's not even mostly between men and women. It's between women and other women.

"On one side, you've got women who never want to be approached by a man. On the other, you've got women who are worried men are just going to stop trying."

If some men do stop trying, that's still a small price to pay for creating a world in which women feel safer and respected. The question is not whether the post-#MeToo world is better. I think we can all agree that it is. The question is how single men and women must adapt to a dating marketplace that's been changed by #MeToo. What are the strategic implications for today's singles?

Up until now, generations of single women have embraced a passive approach to dating better known as "playing hard to get." (*Cambridge Dictionary* definition: "to pretend that you are less interested in someone than you really are as a way of making them more interested in you, especially at the start of a romantic relationship."[3]) Thing is, playing hard to get doesn't work so well in the post-#MeToo world—one where men struggle to decipher which women are playing a game and which women simply wish to be left alone.

For years, playing hard to get has been the philosophy underlying nearly every best-selling dating book written for women. These books teach women that dating is the rare human endeavor in which taking initiative is counterproductive and passivity wins. Rather than encouraging women to be honest with men whom they genuinely like, these books urge women to feign disinterest or dislike and then make men guess whether they want to be pursued or left alone.

"The purpose of the rules," write Ellen Fein and Sherrie Schneider in *The Rules: Time-Tested Secrets for Capturing the Heart of Mr. Right* (1995), "is to make Mr. Right obsessed with having you as his by making yourself seem unattainable."[4]

"If you want a guy to pursue you, don't act so interested," Fein and Schneider write in their 2013 follow-up, *Not Your Mother's Rules*. "Treat him a little bit like a guy you don't care for!"[5]

"If you tell him you are not interested in jumping into a relationship with both feet," Sherry Argov writes in *Why Men Love Bitches* (2002), "he will set out to try to change your mind."[6]

Leslie Braswell's advice in *Ignore the Guy, Get the Guy* (2013) is much the same: "Do not make the mistake of giving him the impression he's on your mind. And it is safe to say if you are talking about him or doing for him, you are thinking of him."[7]

And finally there's Kara King, author of *The Power of the Pussy* (2012). King has a more colorful spin on the same premise: "When you make it hard for a man to get close to you, you become a pussy challenge. There is nothing a man loves more than a pussy challenge!"[8]

Fein, Schneider, and their literary copycats all urge women to be objects of men's affection rather than seekers of it. They berate women who take initiative. God forbid you tell the man you like that you actually like him. The true way to his heart, they claim, is to make him wait four hours for a text-message reply or to tell him you're busy when you're definitely not.

It's a total con—one that essayist Anna North laid bare in a 2009 *Jezebel* article.[9] North, a onetime member of the *New York Times* editorial board, calls out these books for taking "the biggest and dumbest assumptions of evolutionary psychology"—namely that "hunting isn't social, that women didn't hunt, that what men and women may or may not have done in prehistory determines what we do now" (more on this in Chapter 2)—and then repackaging junk science as faux wisdom for desperate singles.

"Society is set up for women to be passive," writes North. "Women are supposed to wait around for this socially-constructed metric of personal success [marriage] to just happen to them. It's no wonder that women seek ways to gain some control over the situation—and self-help books, with their promises of 'bagging the right guy,' offer that control."

Are there some men out there who truly are susceptible to the wiles and mind games advocated by the likes of Fein and Schneider? No doubt. The problem is that there aren't nearly enough such men. And when sex ratios are lopsided, the game-playing approach becomes that much harder for women to pull off.

Of course, dating would be easier if all you had to do to land Mr. Right was ignore him. But that is not the real world. What is real is being true to yourself—leaning into dating the same way you already lean in with career, education, politics, and so much else. Young women are changing the world, yet the dating experts keep telling you that you can't be in charge of your own love lives. Books like *The Rules* and its countless copycats ask you to wait for the man of your choice to simply intuit that

> Of course, dating would be easier if all you had to do to land Mr. Right was ignore him. But that is not the real world.

you want him to ask you out on a date. They urge you to feign disinterest in order to induce men to pursue you.

The message these authors want young women to send to young men: Not interested means keep trying.

This was never a helpful message, but in a post-#MeToo world, it's downright destructive. The overwhelming majority of women do *not* want men to believe that not interested means keep trying. Women want men to take them at their word. "If she's saying she's not interested," New Zealand–based dating coach Caroline Cranshaw counsels men, "get the hint."[10]

Indeed, if #MeToo has taught men anything about dating, it's that good men back off when women rebuff their advances. Persistence in the face of resistance is not sexy. It's harassment. So why then do the rules mavens continue to encourage precisely this sort of persistence?

Francesca Hogi, a high-profile dating coach in Los Angeles, tells me that #MeToo has forced her to rethink the counsel she gives her female clients. The more that men rein in hypermasculine impulses, the harder it becomes for women to win at playing hard to get, she says. On a personal level, Hogi is glad that #MeToo is making the world safer for women, but professionally the new climate has been challenging. It's forcing her to have difficult heart-to-hearts with female clients. Her new message to women: Stop expecting men to chase you.

"If a woman comes across as indifferent," says Hogi, "men will take that as a sign that she's not interested and will move on. It's getting to a point that if the woman doesn't make the first move, the men are not going to."[11]

New challenges for the rule-bound create new opportunities for the rule-breakers. Subtlety is out. Directness is in. Assertive women who are willing to make the first move now have an advantage over rivals who sideline themselves by demanding to be pursued or courted.

"This is not the time to be demure," says Hogi. "At least not if you're single and don't want to be single."

––––––––

Ignoring dating's obsolete rule books is the first step to making your move. Step two is politely declining all the well-intentioned advice you keep getting from moms, aunts, hairdressers, and married pals. No, joining a book club or taking a cooking class is *not* a good way to meet men (though it is a good way to meet other like-minded women!). That story Aunt Suzie likes to tell about how she met Uncle Bob on a singles cruise is about as relevant to 2021 dating as good penmanship is to 2021 writing. Friends and family mean well, but it's time for single women to stop indulging them.

Today's single women know they'd have been proposed to five times over if finding a partner were as simple as joining a book club or going on a singles cruise. Young women understand that dating is harder today than it was for their moms and aunts. Everything about dating has changed, so the conventional wisdom on how to date and whom to date must change too.

Here are a few of the new dating realities:

1. Online dating has turned dating from a mysterious adventure into a daily chore. Tinder users now spend ninety minutes per day on the dating app—and that was before COVID-19 quarantine gave singles

nothing better to do.[12] Instagram users spend thirty minutes by comparison. (My thumb hurts just thinking about this.)

2. Dating apps have eroded singles' one-on-one interpersonal skills. Consider the viral tweet sent out by @SarahGraceEmily in October 2019. Sarah was smitten with a cute guy sitting behind her at a football game. But instead of just turning around and making small talk, Sarah figured that a better way to meet him would be tweeting out a selfie with the guy in the background. Her caption: "everyone help me find this man I saw at the football game, I want to go on a date with him."[13]

3. The workplace, once a hush-hush dating oasis where 20 percent of Americans met their romantic match, has morphed into a dating minefield. The percentage of American couples who meet at work has been cut in half since 1990, according to Stanford University sociologist Michael Rosenfeld.[14] Some men—usually the decent, marriage-material ones—are just too afraid of getting fired (or, worse, getting sent to sexual-harassment training) to even suggest to a female colleague that they go out on a date after work.

4. The rise of Millennial women in the workplace and in higher education is redefining not just the place of women but the place of men too. To put this in *Sex and the City* terms, "badass" is the new "big." Strong women do not need a high-earning man to raise a family in comfort. They aren't looking for a savior. What

they want is an ally or a fellow traveler. A man who doesn't resent their success but embraces it.

This is where conventional dating books start telling today's women to embrace their feminine sides and to stop scaring off men with all their smarts and their job success. As Fein and Schneider instruct in *The Rules*, "Don't overwhelm him with your career triumphs. Try to let him shine!"[15] Translation: It's fine to be a badass at work—just so long as you pretend to be Elle Woods (pre-Harvard Law!) on date night.

Are there still men out there who are scared off by smart, successful women? Of course there are. But the world is changing fast. When Match.com's annual singles survey asked men about their biggest turn-ons for 2016, the number-one answer was "female entrepreneurs."[16]

"It makes sense," says Helen Fisher, Match's chief scientist. "What is an entrepreneur? They're daring, they're creative, they're conscientious."

I'm not so sure about the conscientious part, but entrepreneurs definitely know what they want, and *that* men do find attractive. Ninety-five percent of men want women to ask for men's phone numbers and initiate the first kiss, according to the Match survey. Women are "piling into the job market, gaining economically, and gaining sexually and socially," Fisher says. For men, "feminism has really made dating easier, safer, and more enjoyable for them."

Economic and educational data also support the notion that men and women are increasingly comfortable with shifting gender roles. According the US Bureau of Labor Statistics, women were the sole breadwinners in 38 percent of single-income marriages in 2015, up from 24 percent in 1987.[17] They were the primary breadwinners in 29 percent of dual-income marriages, up from 18 percent. Also, according to the Pew Research Center, there were more men married to better-educated women in 2007 than there were women married to better-educated men.[18]

We've reached an inflection point in modern courtship. Young women are no longer the weaker sex. Millennial and Gen Z women are kicking ass in higher education[19] and emerging as the dominant sex in the workforce.[20] They're finally starting to outearn male peers too. In Boston, for example, the percentage of recent college grads now earning at least $40,000 a year is twice as high for women as for men, according to an Accenture report cited by the *Boston Globe*.[21] Another study—this one commissioned by the white-collar job site Hired—found that entry-level women typically ask for starting salaries 2 percent *higher* than male counterparts and wind up receiving salaries 7 percent higher.[22] The reason young women are successful is because they take initiative. So why the heck would anyone tell them to take the passive approach when it comes to finding love?

Thomas Edwards, a dating coach and professional wingman in Los Angeles, had just finished up a meeting with a female client when I called him for a scheduled phone interview. He told me that his client—very attractive and very mad at him—had bristled at his suggestion that it was time for her to accept the fact that fewer men will make the first move with her. She still wanted the perfect man to seek her out. Edwards kept telling her that times have changed.

"Guys were always afraid of approaching beautiful women," Edwards says. "Now what's happening—and I'd say most of it is irrational—is that the guys worry about being labeled as creepy if they do anything remotely aggressive. I told her she just has to embrace the power of being bold."

Three thousand miles away in New York City, matchmaker Hunt Ethridge has been having similar conversations with his female clientele. "Men who were scared to approach girls before are even more scared now," says Ethridge.

> "Guys were always afraid of approaching beautiful women . . . Now what's happening—and I'd say most of it is irrational—is that the guys worry about being labeled as creepy if they do anything remotely aggressive. I told her she just has to embrace the power of being bold."

Everyone understands that in a perfect world, men would not equate bad pickup lines with the behavior of #MeToo lowlifes like Harvey Weinstein. Women know the difference between the actual creeps and the regular guys who just need a little work on their game. Nevertheless, irrational fears of being labeled a harasser—combined with some perfectly rational responses to women indicating they want to be left alone—have forever changed the way men interact (or don't interact) with women. The end result: It's becoming very hard for women to win at playing hard to get.

Join the Conversation on the
Make Your Move Blog at JonBirger.com

Brian Howie, host of *The Great Love Debate*, chooses Starbucks for his guy-picks-up-girl experiment because people usually go to Starbucks alone. But Brian says his favorite chain store for meeting people is actually Home Depot. According to Brian, "People are in positive, creative moods, and aren't afraid to approach each other to ask for advice or opinion." What's your favorite real-world locale for meeting the opposite sex?

2

SUITOR'S ADVANTAGE

Everyone has their favorite internet time-waster. Mine happens to be AskReddit, a subforum on the social news and discussion website Reddit. Users pose funny, crazy questions, and the answers typically range from thoughtful to hilarious to truly bizarre. It's what makes AskReddit so addictive.

A few years ago, one Redditor posed a dating question that was right up my alley: "Guys of Reddit, what's the most obvious 'hint' from a girl you've missed?"[1] The answers reveal a ton about why men and women who are attracted to one another don't always end up together:

> I had a girl ask me once if I wanted to sleep with her. It was nearly a year later that it occurred to me that she might have been serious.

Her: Want to share a taxi back to my place?

Me: Sure I can drop you off then go home myself. Woke up in the middle of that night and knew exactly what I'd done.

Years ago I was crushing on this girl HARD, for months. She worked for the same company I did, but in a different building, so we rarely had the opportunity to interact . . .

Well, a few days before Christmas one year, she comes waltzing up to me unexpectedly at work, wearing one of those party headbands with a springy plastic mistletoe bouncing around over her head. Says something like, "Hey, what's up. Like my hat?"

"Uh . . . yeah, cute," I say.

"It's mistletoe . . ." she says, with a big shaky grin. "People have been trying to kiss me, can you believe it!"

My dumbass responds with, "Yeah. That sounds pretty inappropriate," like I'm damn Dwight Schrute from *The Office* or something.

She says, "Oh, OK," and hightails it out of the building without looking at another person.

At the time I was a little heartbroken that the girl I thought I liked was the type to just randomly go around asking

(continued on next page)

coworkers to kiss her . . . Didn't occur to me later that I was probably the only person she approached. Shit, she probably went out and got the silly hat specifically to set up that scenario with me because it was clear that I didn't have the balls to make the first move beyond giving her puppy-dog eyes for half a year. The way she shuffled away was like someone punched in the gut.

Idiot.

I'm 22. Playing on a recreational sports team. I would usually drive this one girl on our team home afterwards. On one of the drives, I mentioned that my hands were cold (it was winter). She says, "When my hands are cold, I usually put them between my legs . . . it's always warm down there." I thought about this for a moment, and concluded that my pants were too thick to meaningfully warm my hands . . .

A couple weeks later she tried again with, "Do you have a girlfriend?"

"Nope."

"I can help you with that. ;)"

She got through to me that time.

The AskReddit thread goes on and on like this, with each story more funny and pathetic than the previous one. It makes me think of my own missed-signals story. Coming home from a college party, a woman in my dorm hit the stop button on the elevator with just the two of us in it.

She claimed the elevator was going too fast.

I suggested we take the stairs.

Yes, men are morons.

———

"Yeah, Jon, we already knew that!" you may be thinking. But not so fast, ladies. When it comes to deciphering whether or not someone is flirting, women are just as inept as men.

Jeffrey Hall, a communications studies professor at the University of Kansas, set up an experiment in which fifty-two sets of single, college-aged, heterosexual men and women sat alone in a room and talked one-on-one for ten minutes. The subjects were told the study involved first impressions. Afterward, they were asked to fill out questionnaires in separate rooms, and among the questions was whether or not they had flirted with their partner and whether their partner had flirted with them.

Only 36 percent of men accurately detected that they were being flirted with. The women were even less successful at recognizing flirting. Only 18 percent of women knew when the men were flirting.

"Behavior that is flirtatious is hard to see," Hall says of the results. "People aren't going to do it in obvious ways because they don't want to be embarrassed." If someone is actually interested in you, Hall concludes, "you probably missed it."[2]

The lesson here? Even if you consider yourself a master flirter, the reality is that most of your hair flips and shoe dangles are lost on their intended targets. "Jeez, if I had done a shoe dangle with my husband," my literary agent tells me when I mention Hall's study, "he probably would have thought there was something wrong with my foot."

The ineffectiveness of flirting is why making a real first move is so important. If flirting communicated romantic interest clearly and effectively, everyone would know when they were being flirted with. The flirtation itself would suffice as a first move because the recipient would have no fear of rejection. Unfortunately, flirting does not work this way, which is why singles willing to make genuine first moves tend to be more successful at dating. Remember all those pathetic AskReddit stories? The only woman who ultimately got her guy was the one who stopped flirting and took the direct approach: *"Do you have a girlfriend?"* . . . *"Nope."* . . . *"I can help you with that."*

> The ineffectiveness of flirting is why making a clear first move is so important. If flirting communicated romantic interest effectively, everybody would know when they were being flirted with.

Here's what I want you to take away from all this: It's better to choose than be chosen. I call this "suitor's advantage," and this is more than just my own pet theory. It's the only dating strategy ever awarded a Nobel Prize. And no, I'm not kidding.

In 2012, American economists Alvin Roth and Lloyd Shapley won the Nobel Prize in Economics for their work on what became known as the "stable marriage" or "stable matching" problem. (Roth developed practical applications for economic theories first formulated by Shapley and by Shapley's colleague David Gale in 1961.) There's a nice summary of Roth and Shapley's research on the Nobel website,[3] but the short version is this: When it comes to traditional forms of matching—dating, hiring, school admissions, and the like—the party that initiates the match typically achieves a better outcome than the party on the receiving end.

In Shapley and Gale's original thought experiment, they proposed a scenario in which there were ten men and ten women who all wanted to get married, but only one sex could propose. In Shapley and Gale's experiment, it was the men who could propose marriage. Women ranked the men in terms of their desirability as marriage partners, and the men did the same for the women. Then each man proposed marriage to "his favorite girl."[4]

If a woman received a proposal from her first-choice man, the happy couple could start planning the wedding. But if her first proposal came from a man who was lower ranked on her list, she would then demur and hope for a better offer. "She does not accept him yet," Shapley and Gale explain, "but keeps him on a string to allow for the possibility that something better may come along." The risk, of course, is that he will find someone else before she ever gets the chance to pull on that string.

The experiment then proceeds to stage two. "Those boys who have been rejected now propose to their second choice," they write. "Each girl receiving proposals chooses her favorite from the group consisting of the new proposals and the boy on her string, if any. She rejects all the rest and again keeps the favorite in suspense. We proceed in the same manner. Those who are rejected at the second stage propose to their next choices, and the girls again reject all but the best proposal they have had so far."

The process then continues until we arrive at the point at which there's no longer any man or woman without a match. I won't run through all the fancy math, but what Shapley and Gale ultimately prove is that whichever sex initiates the matches (in this case the men) will end up with higher-ranked matches, on average, than the sex on the receiving end (in this case the women). "When the boys propose, the result is optimal for the boys, and when the girls propose, it is optimal for the girls," Shapley and Gale conclude.

That is suitor's advantage in a nutshell. It's better to choose than be chosen. Women like my friend Sam have an advantage because their assertiveness guarantees them a shot with their first-choice men. For women who wait to be asked out on dates, there is no such guarantee because guys don't always know which women are interested in them.

Not that Nobel laureates require much affirmation, but a 2015 OkCupid study reached a similar conclusion.[5] OkCupid found that women who make the first move with men end up with more attractive partners than those who sit back and wait for men to message them. "When women are proactive,"

OkCupid chief product officer Jimena Almendares explains to ABC News, "there's a big win."[6]

I know what the rule-followers reading this are thinking: "But I've been told that bad things happen to women who pursue men! That human evolution pre-programs men to chase women, not the other way around!" In a 2013 interview with the *Times* of London, *The Rules* authors Ellen Fein and Sherrie Schneider went so far as to blame the fictional dating woes of the young women in the HBO series *Girls* on these characters' failure to follow their own rules.

"Our strength is quiet and powerful: it doesn't come from being aggressive," Schneider says. Fein chimes in: "Women can chase apartments and jobs, but not men. It's biology."[7]

> There is no biological imperative for men to chase women and for women to play hard to get.

The notion that biology hardwires men to chase and women to play catch-me-if-you-can is so ingrained in popular culture that I understand why Fein, Schneider, and their followers simply assumed it to be true. Conventional wisdom rarely gets fact-checked, unfortunately, and in this instance, blind faith gave rise to a literary genre built largely on junk science. Fein, Schneider, and their disciples were hoodwinked by a now-debunked scientific narrative. A generation of single women paid the price.

Simply put, there is no biological imperative for men to chase women and for women to play hard to get. The way men and women approach courtship and relationships has more to do with prevailing culture than with our DNA. When culture changes, behavior once considered immutable often changes along with it.

That last line is a paraphrase from a 2017 book that is a must-read for anyone interested in the science of gender and mate choice. The book is *Inferior: How Science Got Women Wrong—and the New Research That's Rewriting the Story* by Angela Saini, an award-winning science journalist based in London. Saini's book pulverizes old stereotypes about women being hardwired to be passive. What Saini calls "the myth of the coy, passive female"[8] isn't just hopelessly sexist but also demonstrably wrong—so wrong that it's rather baffling how the research behind it ever got elevated to canon in the first place.

———

Saini's story of how science got women wrong begins with a fruit fly.

In 1948, British botanist Angus John Bateman performed an experiment that tested one of Charles Darwin's theories from *The Descent of Man.* Darwin believed that males chase multiple females in hopes of maximizing offspring, whereas females' best reproductive strategy was always to fend off most suitors while waiting for the very best male specimens to come their way. Bateman chose fruit flies for his study because fruit flies reproduce quickly and have mutations that make it easy to identify parentage. Bateman observed that male fruit flies were always the sexual aggressors and also that 20 percent of male fruit flies produced no offspring compared to just 4 percent of the females. His findings seemed to confirm Darwin's original hypothesis that females succeed genetically by being passive and choosy, even if that means sharing an alpha-male mate with other females.

Bateman's fruit fly research received scant attention at the time it was published. It might have been forgotten to history were it not rediscovered by a young Harvard University researcher by the name of Robert Trivers. Today Trivers is considered by many to be the most influential evolutionary biologist of his generation, even though his career has seen its share of controversy. Here's how Trivers once justified accepting research grants from sex-offender financier Jeffrey Epstein: "By the time [girls are] fourteen or fifteen, they're like grown women were sixty years ago, so I don't see these acts as so heinous."[9]

It's entirely possible that conventional dating guides like *The Rules* would never have become best sellers were it not for Trivers's influence.[10] Without the intellectual cover he and his protégés (almost all men) provided for the play-hard-to-get crowd, Fein, Schneider, and the other rules mavens would have had a harder time arguing that biology hardwires men to chase and women to be passive filters of male advances.

In *Inferior*, Saini interviews Trivers about how he first discovered Bateman's original article, "Intra-Sexual Selection in *Drosophila*." Suffice it to say that the interview does not go well for him. Trivers tells Saini that he had been studying the mating patterns of pigeons (particularly those pigeons outside his office window) when a colleague told him about Bateman's research and encouraged him to look it up. "He remembers it with graphic clarity," Saini writes of Trivers. "He went to the museum to photocopy it, 'with my testicles pressed firmly against the side of the Xerox machine,' he tells me, with a throaty laugh. As soon as he read it, 'The scales fell from my eyes.'"[11]

Based on Bateman's study, Trivers concluded that female fruit flies—and by extension females of other species too—have little incentive to be sexually assertive or to have sex with multiple partners. "A female's reproductive success did not increase much, if any, after the first copulation and not at all after the second," Trivers writes.[12]

It wasn't long before a whole new generation of academics—David Buss, Geoffrey Miller, Steven Pinker, Don Symons, among others—was building upon Trivers's ideas, all of them advancing a sexual selection theory promoting the belief that "men are promiscuous and undiscriminating while women are highly discriminating and sexually passive," according to Saini.[13]

There was just one problem. The science was wrong.

Patricia Gowaty, an evolutionary biologist at the University of California, Los Angeles, had spent the first part of her career studying the mating patterns of eastern bluebirds. Her findings didn't jibe with theories put forth by Bateman and Trivers and their many acolytes. Gowaty had found that female bluebirds—once thought to be seasonally monogamous—were actually flying away at night to mate with males that were not their primary partners.

Male colleagues dismissed Gowaty's research as amateurish, according to Saini. They told Gowaty that the female bluebirds in her study must have been "raped."

Gowaty was not discouraged. She decided to repeat Bateman's original fruit fly experiment and see if the female fruit flies really were as passive as Bateman had claimed. She and three colleagues replicated Bateman's experiment exactly as he described it—yet came up with entirely different results. Videotapes showed the females to be just as sexually assertive as the males. Female fruit flies moved toward males just as often as males moved toward females.

Gowaty found other errors too. For instance, Bateman had overestimated the number of male flies with no mates. He had also made the rather bizarre error of counting mothers as parents more than fathers—"a biological impossibility," Saini writes, "since it takes two to make a baby."[14] Finally, Bateman overlooked the biological inevitability that utilizing flies with mutations would lead to lower survival rates among fertilized eggs with double mutations—a big problem considering that Bateman had used presence of offspring as his only evidence of mating. The mistakes were so egregious that Gowaty wondered whether Bateman's editor had actually read the study.

"Far from being passive, coy, and monogamous . . . females of many species have been shown to be active, powerful, and very willing to mate with more than one male."

To be clear, Gowaty has never asserted that no species behave as Bateman and Trivers suggest. Her critique is that the theories put forth by Bateman and Trivers are like a box and that new research shows fewer and fewer species fitting into that box. And that includes humans. "Far from being passive, coy, and monogamous," Saini summarizes, "females of many species have been shown to be active, powerful, and very willing to mate with more than one male."[15]

To illustrate how all this applies to humans, Saini cites a dramatic example—the polyamorous Himba society of northern Namibia. In Himba society, all married women possess the sexual freedom to carry on affairs with any men of their choosing.

I have nothing against polyamory, and I do not believe traditional marriage is for everyone. Nevertheless, as I was reading Saini's colorful stories about the sexual practices of Himba women, it occurred to me that there is another example from modern anthropology that might illustrate Gowaty's point in a manner more relatable for my own readers—single, marriage-minded, college-educated women. That example is the Bijago culture of Orango Island, off the coast of Guinea-Bissau in West Africa.

Bijago women are the world's original badasses. Historically, only the women in Bijago society are allowed to propose marriage.[16] The woman does so by preparing a distinctive seafood dish marinated in palm oil and then presenting it to the man she wishes to marry. It's the Bijago equivalent of a man getting down on one knee and offering a ring to the woman he hopes will become his wife.

In an interview with the Associated Press, Orango Island resident Carvadju Jose Nananghe recalls fondly the story of his own wife's surprise proposal.

"I had no feelings for her [beforehand]," says Nananghe, then sixty-five. "Then when I ate this meal, it was like lightning. I wanted only her."[17]

When asked if he'd ever considered choosing his own wife, Nananghe seems baffled.

"Love comes first into the heart of the woman," he says. "Once it's in the woman, only then can it jump into the man."

In recent years, the Bijagos' gender-bending courtship culture has been challenged by economic forces. Orango Island men have been traveling to mainland Africa to sell palm oil and to work for tourist resorts. When they return home, the men bring with them mainland ideas about dating—namely that men are supposed to chase women. This worries Orango Island elders. As one of them tells the AP, whenever men propose to women, the marriages seem less likely to last.

"The choice of a woman is much more stable . . . Rarely were there divorces before. Now, with men choosing, divorce has become common."

"The choice of a woman is much more stable," says ninety-year-old Cesar Okrane. "Rarely were there divorces before. Now, with men choosing, divorce has become common."

Bijago women are fierce, though, especially when it comes to preserving their traditions. Just ask twenty-three-year-old Laurindo Carvalho. Carvalho had worked at the resorts as a teenager, and he admitted feeling the pull of mainland culture.

He had been lusting after a certain girl in his village, so one day he decided to ask her to marry him.

She rejected him with a wave of her hand.

Then six years passed.

One day he heard a knock on his door. It was the love of his life, with a plate of fish and a smile on her face.

Says Carvalho, "I learned the hard way that here, a man never approaches a woman."

———

I left something out of the Bijago story, something important about their culture. Something relevant to the rise of Millennial and Gen Z women in Western culture. On Orango Island, it's not just dating and marriage that are controlled by women. It is the entire social structure. Bijago society is matriarchal, which means women control not just marriage customs but the economy and the laws too.

"It is [women] who impose sanctions, direct . . . and distribute goods, and they are respected as the absolute owners of both the house and the land," according to a 2015 article in the African news magazine *VozAfric*. "Here it is the man who has the obligation to dress very well to attract the attention of a woman. Women hold the supreme power of divorce in marriage. Men are turned to only for the tilling of the fields, hunting monkeys, and fishing."[18]

No, I'm not suggesting that the rise of young women in the West is leading us toward a matriarchal society exactly like the one that exists on Orango Island. My point is merely that dating and mating are influenced by the broader culture. Young women in the United States are leaving men behind when it comes to education, and historically there's been a correlation between education and earnings. The college gender gap is sufficiently wide nowadays that Millennial and Gen Z women will almost certainly be their generations' high earners (and that's even with men getting paid more for the same work). If sex roles are shifting in our classrooms, in our workplaces, and in our halls of government, it's inevitable that they're going to shift in our dating culture too.

When it comes to mating patterns, biology is not immutable. Biology and culture are intertwined. In the animal kingdom, there are bird species such as jacanas and red phalaropes for which sex roles are reversed—males are pursued by hyperaggressive females. Not only do female jacanas spar over males, but they also try to mate with as many males as possible. The scientific explanation for why jacanas have reversed sex roles is tied to hormones. Female jacanas have unusually high levels of testosterone, whereas male jacanas have unusually low levels. Scientists believe these hormone levels influence which sex takes the lead role in mating.

This has implications for humans. Conventional wisdom has long held that men are hardwired to be aggressive—to pursue women, wealth, power, and so on—and that testosterone makes men this way. But a new study led by Sari van Anders, a professor of psychology, neuroscience, and gender studies at Queen's University in Ontario, has raised doubts about whether this is true. Gender roles and dating behavior may be tied to testosterone levels, but van Anders's team found that those levels can vary depending upon circumstance and situation: "We found that wielding power increased testosterone in women compared with a control, regardless of whether it was performed in gender-stereotyped masculine or feminine ways."[19]

The mere act of engaging in "competitive behavior" leads to higher testosterone levels, according to the study, whereas the avoidance of competitive situations has the opposite effect.

"Accordingly, cultural pushes for men to wield power and [for] women to avoid doing so may partially explain, in addition to heritable factors, why testosterone levels tend to be higher in men than in women," writes van Anders. "A lifetime of gender socialization could contribute to 'sex differences' in testosterone."

Van Anders's research focuses on women, but a much-publicized 2007 article in the *Journal of Clinical Endocrinology and Metabolism* observed a corresponding *decline* in men's testosterone.[20] Men nowadays are more invested in parenting than were men of prior generations, and studies show that male testosterone declines when men spend more time with their families and less time golfing, hunting, or generally socializing with other men.[21]

Depending on your personal politics, the social forces at play here represent either progress or apocalypse. The so-called feminization of the American male has become a culture-war obsession for extremists on the right,[22] whereas the quest to ban "toxic masculinity" has become a cause célèbre for many on the left.

"Men have been beaten down, beaten down, beaten down, and gosh, a lot of men have become sissies," right-wing ideologue Ann Coulter said in a 2017 interview.[23]

"We do a great disservice to boys in how we raise them," counters author Chimamanda Ngozi Adichie in her 2015 essay *We Should All Be Feminists*. "We stifle the humanity of boys. We define masculinity in a very narrow way. Masculinity is a hard, small cage, and we put boys inside this cage. We teach boys to be afraid of fear, of weakness, of vulnerability."[24]

I generally side with Adichie on this one (though I do wish others on the left were as thoughtful on this subject as she is). I don't see anything wrong with men being nurturing—I have been the lead parent in my own family. Nor do I see the testosterone studies as some sort of red flag portending cultural doom. That said, the goal of *Make Your Move* is not to take sides in a culture war but to address strategic implications and solutions for single, hetero women seeking their partners in a changed world.

We know that men are being socialized differently today than they were twenty or thirty years ago. Colleges are promoting sensitivity programs that explicitly tamp down on traditional masculinity and encourage men to show more "vulnerability."[25] During freshman orientation at Gettysburg College, for example, students are shown a film in which they're told that "the three most destructive words" every man hears when he's a boy are "be a man."[26]

Thing is, socialization is a two-way street. Just as young men have been socialized to be tough and take-charge, young women have been socialized to desire men who possess those same traits. In a 2018 study, researchers Pelin Gul and Tom R. Kupfer of Iowa State University and the University of Kent, respectively, found that while women do appreciate woke or pro-feminist men in the workplace, they generally do not favor such men as romantic partners. Women give higher rankings, on average, to traditional men with "benevolently sexist" attitudes—men who believe, for example, that women are vulnerable and less capable and thus must be helped and protected. The finding is even true for college-age women who self-identify as feminists, according to Gul and Kupfer. Their explanation? Benevolently sexist men are deemed more attractive because women perceive them as most likely to "protect, provide and commit." Other men notice this preference and behave accordingly. "Men's benevolent sexism may often be motivated by mating concerns," the researchers conclude, "because if women favor men who display benevolence, there will be considerable advantages for men who behave in this way."[27]

In other words, there's a reason John Wayne has been considered sexy and Fred Rogers has not. (There are exceptions, of course: "I have unclean thoughts about Mr. Rogers," confesses relationship blogger Dixie Laite of Dametown.com. "After rocking his world, I'd cuddle in close while Mr. Rogers tells me he 'loves me just the way I am' as he falls asleep, off to dream about pie and brotherhood and helping sad, lonely children."[28]) Today's men are still sorting out when it's okay to be brave and assertive and when it's not. Teaching young men to reject masculinity and embrace vulnerability will not mold John Waynes—which is probably a good thing. John Wayne would put his arm around any darned dame he fancied. Actually, he would do far more than that—spanking Elizabeth Allen in *Donovan's Reef* (1963)[29] and forcibly kissing Maureen O'Hara in *The Quiet Man* (1952)[30] as she was trying to flee. Today, such behavior wouldn't just be over-the-top inappropriate—it would be criminal.

As a parent of three boys, I want young men to be respectful toward women. I want them to be aware that certain words and actions will be perceived differently by women than they will by other men. If that means reining in traditional masculinity—even in ways that may seem excessive—so be it.

Still, with any societal shift, there will always be unintended consequences. My fear with this one is that Millennials and Gen Z-ers will never get to experience all the little acts of intimacy that require some risk-taking but can be so thrilling in the moment—and so important to cultivating deeper connections over time.

He reaches out to hold his date's hand in a movie, and she responds by running her index finger slowly up and down his palm. He puts his arm around her at a party, and she leans in instead of leaning out. He touches her hair, and she responds by touching his face.

These little acts of physicality used to be staples of courtship. They were often preludes to a first kiss (with good reason, since flirtatious touching releases hormones that promote trust and inhibit stress[31]). Nowadays, however, it can be harder for a man to put his arm around a date than it is for him to ask matter-of-factly if she wants to go back to his apartment for sex. Traditional romance is being replaced by the transactional sterility of online dating.

I find this sad, though I do see remedies. One involves applying to hand-holding and half-hugs the same standards of consent we commonly apply to sex and to other more intimate forms of physicality. It's the safest option—and perhaps where our culture is headed—though it's not terribly romantic. Indeed, a web survey conducted by Dr. Duana Welch of the *Love Science* blog found that 64 percent of women do not want men to ask for verbal consent before initiating a first kiss (which, of course, is far more intimate than holding hands).[32] Women whom Welch surveyed preferred that men not ruin the moment and just pick up on physical cues instead—though, as we've learned, the latter is more art than science.

"I think it ruins the mood," one young woman says of men who ask permission before initiating a first kiss. "I want someone who is able to read my body language." (Most of the women in Welch's survey were between the ages of eighteen and thirty-four.)

Says another: "If the guy asks, it makes him look weak. If he does it without permission, it makes him look like he's assertive, like he knows what he wants in life and is not afraid to go after it. But this only applies to kissing, not other things."

"No," says a third, "I think that being asked takes the excitement and romance out of the first kiss. The moments leading up to the kiss are sometimes the most exciting, and if you know it's coming it wouldn't be nearly as fun."

These are complicated conversations, and I have no idea where the consensus will land. But I do see an alternative solution, one that bypasses the problem altogether: Women can take the lead. Unwanted advances can be intimidating for women, simply because men tend to be bigger and stronger. Not so when the roles are reversed. As Hogi, the LA dating coach, puts it: "For men, the physical touch of a woman is almost always welcome."

Real human biology is not the biology of *The Rules*. If testosterone levels are tied to gender roles and if testosterone levels are falling in men and rising in women, men will be less inclined—maybe even less equipped—to be suitors. Women will be more so. If more women are taking leadership roles in business and politics, it's inevitable that more women will start taking the lead in romance too. Just like those badass Bijago women.

So here's the bottom line. If that cute guy in accounting is ignoring all your flirty body language, don't automatically assume that he's not interested. Maybe he's oblivious. Maybe he's just nervous.

Or maybe he's just waiting for you to do something bolder than dangle a shoe.

**Join the Conversation on the
Make Your Move Blog at JonBirger.com**

Bijago women propose by presenting their men with a seafood dish cooked in palm oil. If your beloved were to propose to you with food, what would be the perfect dish?

3

MEN LIKE WOMEN WHO LIKE THEM

Evie has a secret.

Evie's friends all think she's happily married. And she is. Sort of. What her friends do not know, however, is that Evie—a thirty-four-year-old management consultant in Boston—also has a boyfriend on the side. Not only that, but her husband, Patrick, knows all about him.

Evie and Patrick decided to open up their marriage two years ago. She began dating a man she knew from work, and now the three of them—Evie, Patrick, and boyfriend Seth—are making some very brave-new-world plans to raise a child together in a three-parent family.

And that will require some serious 'splainin' to her friends, all of whom believe she and Patrick have a conventional marriage.

"I'm dreading it," Evie says of telling her friends.

Evie's fear is not so much that her friends will be judgmental about her polyamorous lifestyle. Evie's friends are just as open-minded and liberal as she is. The real issue is that her closest friends are single women in their thirties who really want to get married but just can't seem to find the right guy.

"I literally feel like they're going to lunge across the table and stab me once they find out that I've got two men of marriage age who love me, both with incredible looks and incredible qualifications," Evie confesses.

The reason I'm sharing Evie's story is not because I'm endorsing polyamory as some sort of newfangled dating strategy. Like I said, I'm agnostic on the monogamy versus polyamory debate. The reason I'm introducing you to Evie is because this chapter is a how-to on making the first move with the men of your choice. And Evie happens to be a master practitioner.

What the stories of Evie and other badass daters you'll meet here will show is that making the first move never requires a woman to throw herself at a man. It never demands from women the same sort of over-the-top persistence that the rules mavens demand from men. It certainly doesn't mean having sex before you (or he, for that matter) are ready.

Evie and other badass daters just know things that you may not. Lesson number one: Men like women who like them.

To men, this is perfectly obvious. Whenever I use this line on the lecture circuit, the men in the audience usually nod in unison. Women, however, seem dubious. They've been taught the exact opposite. Their moms, sisters, and best friends have them convinced that men love being ignored and having their advances rebuffed. They believe men can't truly be happy with a woman unless she presents herself as unattainable and then makes him chase her and jump through countless hoops in order to earn her affection.

This is why rule-follower women feel blindsided every time a rule-breaker like Evie nabs a man simply by being direct and honest.

Lesson number two is that making the first move doesn't have to be scary. It's so much easier for women to make their move than it is for men. For women, all it requires is giving a man the green light. He'll take it from there. It never means sacrificing your femininity. While first moves by men tend to be bold or brazen, women's can be sweet and playful. When done correctly, a first move by a woman never requires the bluster and hypermasculinity that society has come to expect from our alpha-male suitors.

> Making the first move doesn't have to be scary. It's so much easier for women to make their move than it is for men. For women, all it requires is giving a man the green light. He'll take it from there.

Now back to Evie. I need you to know that Evie is attractive but not head-turningly so. She doesn't wear much makeup, and her wardrobe is more L.L.Bean than Chanel. I wrote and rewrote those sentences a few times because I am wary (as all men should be) of ranking women by their attractiveness. But in this instance I think it's important for women reading

Evie's story to have some sense of what she looks like. I want you focused on her approach. I do not want you wondering whether she looks like Rihanna and thinking, "Well, maybe that's why she's so good with men."

Evie's success is all about attitude and confidence. She's naturally assertive in life, so she's naturally assertive with men. Not once has it ever occurred to her that those two things shouldn't go hand in hand.

"My dad used to say, 'Yeah, you're smart but really what you are is tenacious,'" Evie tells me. "I've always been the kind of person who just goes for it when I see something I want."

Evie grew up in Massachusetts, and during her freshman year in high school she decided she wanted to attend an Ivy League university. Not only did Evie commit herself to getting straight As in school and taking as many Advanced Placement classes as possible, but she also decided to join her high school rowing team—never mind that she'd never rowed crew before in her life. Evie took up rowing simply because she believed (correctly, as it turned out) that rowing could help her get into an Ivy League school.

"I actually hated crew," she says. "I was exhausted all the time, but just for motivation, I'd do things like put up rowing posters in my bathroom."

Fortunately for Evie, making the first move with her husband, Patrick, proved far easier than waking up at 5 AM for crew practice.

Evie was twenty-five when she met Patrick. A first-year MBA student at the time, she had just returned home for Thanksgiving break. While home, she made plans to catch up with an old pal—a high school friend who had just come out to her as gay—at the Starbucks in her local Barnes & Noble.

"I'm walking around Barnes & Noble with [my friend] Tommy, and he looks up and says, 'Oh, Patrick Hadley is here—have you ever met Patrick?'"

Evie and Patrick had actually gone to the same high school, and she vaguely knew his sister. But Patrick was three years older, and Evie and Patrick had never met.

"I was pretty jazzed up on coffee, as I remember," Evie recalls. "We went over to say hi. He was there with his mother, doing some Christmas shopping, and I introduced myself. The whole time I was making intense eye contact with him and smiling."

Evie and Tommy eventually said goodbye to Patrick and his mother, and then everyone walked away. A few moments later, Evie asked Tommy if she could borrow his phone—which she then used to send Patrick a text.

"Evie thinks you're really cute!" she wrote.

"I had nothing else to do at home and I was bored out of my mind," Evie recalls. "My thought at the time was 'Oh, he's really cute, maybe this could be a fun thing that I could have for one night and never see this person again.'"

———

Let's pause here and take stock. Evie's goal was to simply make it clear to Patrick that she was interested in him. Whatever happened next was up to Patrick. She did not chase him or throw herself at him—which, of course, is the visual that the rule-followers always conjure up any time somebody suggests that a woman make the first move with a man. All Evie did is open the door wide enough to make Patrick feel confident about walking through. By sending Patrick a harmless little text—from someone else's phone, no less—Evie removed whatever fear of rejection Patrick might have had.

————

Okay, back to the story.

Patrick quickly texted back. "I think Evie is really cute too!" he wrote.

"At this point," says Evie, "Tommy is like, 'Get me the fuck off of this train wreck, you can text him on your own!'

"I'm all excited that he thinks I'm cute, so I texted him [from my own phone] and we made some plans."

They arranged to go out for a beer together the following night, and it turned into your typical Thanksgiving weekend bar crawl—everyone catching up with old friends and drinking a bit too much in the process. Evie spent most of the night talking to her high school friends and Patrick to his. They barely said a word to each other at the bar, but at the end of the night she asked him for a ride home.

"He gave me a ride home in his mom's car. We sat in the car and talked in my parents' driveway like we were in high school for maybe twenty minutes."

It was obvious to Evie that Patrick was too shy to make the first move. "He's just super, super hesitant," she says.

"So I kissed him. We made out in his mom's car for like an hour. Then I got out of the car, and I said, 'Goodbye, Patrick. It was nice knowing you. I guess I'll never see you again.'"

Patrick lived in Portland, Maine, at the time, and Evie was living in Boston. "It just didn't seem like it would ever work out," says Evie.

While Evie did not expect to see Patrick again, she admits she wasn't totally shocked when Patrick kept texting her. Men, she says, have always been turned on by her assertiveness.

"I've always asked men out on dates—that was always my MO," she says. "I don't think I'm fabulous looking or anything, but I've never, ever had any problem with men."

It wasn't long before texts turned into phone calls, which turned into weekend visits. Evie started visiting Patrick semiregularly in Maine; he'd do the same with her in Boston. Next thing she knew, they were in a serious long-distance relationship.

"It was kind of low expectations at first," she recalls. "But I think we said 'I love you' to each other over email within a month of that first date. I actually said it first."

I interrupt Evie to point out that dating traditionalists would say she was crazy to tell a man she loved him before he said it first. Especially after only a month. I even share with her some advice on this topic from the various dating rule books.

From *The Rules*: "He should be the first to say, 'I love you.' He should be an open book, you should be a mystery."[1]

From *Why Men Love Bitches*: "Men automatically assume that, if you're interested, you'll do anything to 'nail him down.'

He immediately thinks you want 'exclusivity'; you want to break open the hope chest and have babies with him."[2]

Evie was aghast.

"Oh god, that never happened. I remember it specifically. We were having a text conversation. I told him I loved him. He said something like 'I just got a warm feeling all over hearing you say that.' He told me he loved me too."

In the case of Seth, her new boyfriend, Evie tried conventional flirting, but it didn't get her anywhere—probably because she was married and he was coming off a divorce. "So I sent him a text saying that 'I think I'm falling in like with you,'" she says. "That was how it started."

At first, Seth assumed Evie was just looking for something casual, but she made it clear that she wanted more than that: "I was very blunt with him. I told him, 'We have this great bond. I like you and I care about you, and I want to be in a relationship with you.'"

During our interview, Evie was always wary of sounding egotistical. My questioning forced her to be highly introspective, but she's not actually the kind of person who goes around telling people how good she is with men. That said, Evie truly believes that her dating success is simply an outgrowth of her natural assertiveness. She's confident and decisive in life, so why not be the same way with men?

"It's all about authenticity, when there's nothing between you and your true self and what you're feeling and thinking,"

Evie says. "Yes, authenticity makes you vulnerable, but like I said, guys seem to like it."

<hr/>

My friend Becca is another woman who's never afraid to make the first move.

A twenty-nine-year-old nurse, Becca is very attractive, and she's something of a character too. (Picture everyone's favorite babysitter—the one who bakes cupcakes, makes baking-soda volcanos, empties closets for crazy dress-up games that include the dog, and then leaves the house an absolute mess—but the parents don't mind because the kids have so much fun and are completely worn out and ready for bed by 9:30 . . . And yes, Becca was our Saturday-night sitter for years.)

While Becca may be an alpha, she's never been particularly attracted to her alpha-male counterparts. She prefers the quirkier, artsier types. Problem is, because of her good looks and big personality, those guys sometimes assume she's way out of their league.

Becca learned early on that she could not wait for guys she likes to make the first move. If she didn't make it 100 percent

"I knew he really liked me, but he had no idea what to do. So I just said to him, 'Hey, are you going to ask for my number?' My god, was he happy! It was like I had removed this huge burden."

clear that she was interested in them, they'd just assume she was being nice.

"I met my current boyfriend at a Super Bowl party. I knew he really liked me, but he had no idea what to do. So I just said to him, 'Hey, are you going to ask for my number?'

"My god, was he happy! It was like I had removed this huge burden."

And that is your goal. Just make it easier for the guy. Becca didn't have to grab his butt or buy him a beer or even ask him out on a proper date. All she had to do was make it clear that she would go out with him if he asked. He took it from there.

It sounds simple enough, but opening this door is something most women still refuse to do. As a result, Becca gets the guys she wants, guys she'd never get if she stuck to the rules. "Girls like us," she says, "have a big advantage."

Is there risk of rejection when women like Becca make the first move? Of course there is. Taking any type of risk means accepting the possibility of failure or a bruised ego. Even Becca acknowledges it would be easier to just wait for some guy to ask her out.

But why settle for some guy?

Today's hottest dating app—Bumble—promotes, exploits, and profits off this concept. On Bumble, only women can initiate online conversations, which means Bumble requires women to make the first move. Whitney Wolfe, Bumble's founder, argues that women do better when they take initiative.

"Generally speaking," Wolfe tells the *Atlantic*, "women my age have been raised with the notion that they are meant to sit put and not make the first move in a relationship and to kind of wait to be courted." She says they are expected to "delicately laugh at [a man's] jokes and just exist in his world."[3]

Such rules make no sense, Wolfe says: "Follow these rules of society, [and] you lose confidence. You lose a sense of yourself . . . If you want something, you have to go out and get it. I've tried the other way—waiting around for something to land in my lap—and it doesn't work."

Wolfe even hired the most badass woman on the planet— tennis megastar Serena Williams—to get out Bumble's message.

"The world tells you to wait," says Serena in Bumble's 2019 Super Bowl commercial. "That waiting is polite. And good things will just come. But if I waited to be invited in, I never would have stood out. If I waited for change to happen, I never would have made a difference. So make the first move. Don't wait to be told your place. Take it. Don't wait for people to find you. Find them."[4]

I'm not a huge fan of online dating (a topic I'll explore more fully in the next chapter). Spending ninety minutes a day swiping and sorting through random dating profiles strikes me as a tough way to meet a partner, especially if there are singles in the real world whom you already know, like, and are attracted to. That said, I do have a soft spot for Bumble. And it's not just because Wolfe is a *Date-onomics* reader who has highlighted my book in press interviews.

I admire Wolfe for recognizing and capitalizing on women's desire for more control over their dating lives. In order to illustrate this desire, Bumble has been compiling and promoting the stories of women who made the first move with their partners.[5] What's clear from the stories is that these women's relationships never would have gotten off the ground had the women not taken the initiative.

Consider the story of Jana, a thirty-three-year-old mother of two and a Bumble interviewee. Jana met her husband, Colin, in college and liked him from the get-go. They spent a year in the friend zone, however, and Jana eventually got tired of waiting for Colin to step up.

"I just realized that it wasn't going to happen on his end," says Jana. "So I thought, 'What do I have to lose?'"

Jana cornered Colin at a party and said, "I want to kiss you. I don't know if you know this but I have a total crush on you."

"He had no idea," Jana says, "and I don't know if it would have ever happened if I didn't make a move . . . If you want something, go after it. You write your own story."

Note that there was nothing masculine about Jana's approach. Her first move was not physical or overly aggressive. All she did was tell Colin how she felt.

Angelique, twenty-six, a television producer in LA and another of Bumble's first-move success stories, took a similar approach. She asked out an older colleague at work (more on office romances in Chapter 6), and they've now been together for several years.

"Making the first move taught me to trust my instincts," Angelique says. "There's been nothing more empowering for me than learning that it's okay to make the first move. And that it doesn't mean you're 'throwing yourself at a guy.' It just means that you're stepping into your power as a woman to make decisions about who and what you want."

Faye, another Bumble interviewee, observes that making the first move online requires less courage than doing so in person.

"Making the first move on a dating app didn't bother me," says Faye. "It's just a matter of saying 'Hi' and chatting, though I'd never go up to a guy in a bar like that. I'm too shy. When I connected with Stu, I just said, 'Hi Stu, how are you doing?'— and it went on from there. I realized that it doesn't have to be a big deal.

"It's as simple as saying hi."

The irony is that "simply saying hi" doesn't work nearly so well when men are the ones saying it. Indeed, a popular pastime on women's dating blogs involves women griping about men who use "hi" or "hey" as openers.

"If you exert so little effort on developing your first impression, how will you behave on a date?" wonders dating blogger Messy Mentor.[6]

"I hate men who say hi with a smile," writes Lisa Zhang on the *Girls Ask Guys* blog. "It's like WHAT? You want some reward and cookies for being 'legally' polite and making me have to deal with you?"[7]

Thing is, the same opener that's such a turnoff for women can have a hypnotizing effect on men. Want a visual? Head over to my website, JonBirger.com, to watch the commercial titled "Firsts" for Anheuser-Busch's Shock Top craft beer. There's a ton of interesting messaging going on here, all of it aimed at young, educated women. But the part I find most significant occurs at the fifteen-second mark, when the commercial's protagonist—a young woman attending a backyard house party—spots a cute guy who may or may not be there with a date. (He's involved in a four-way conversation with another man and two women.)

After making eye contact, the young woman walks purposefully across the backyard—the camera is trained on her feet—stops in front of the man, smiles, and then just says hi. In the commercial, this simple act of saying hi leads to a whirlwind romance involving camping, carnivals, and exotic food. The commercial ends with the happy couple moving in together. If this weren't a beer commercial, the tagline could well have been "the power of simply saying hi."

———

"I don't really understand this fear of coming off as too available or too needy," says Maya, a thirty-two-year-old financial analyst in New York City. Maya had been dating her current boyfriend for eight months when I interviewed her.

I met Maya through one of her friends, a *Date-onomics* reader who came to one of my book talks and sought me out afterward. What started out as this woman peppering me with dating questions soon evolved into a conversation about her friend Maya. She was confused about why Maya had more success with men than she did, despite the fact that Maya was no supermodel.

Curious, I asked her to contact Maya and see if Maya would agree to an interview. She did, and Maya said she'd meet with me.

"She doesn't listen to me," Maya would later say about the friend.

As with all the badass daters I interviewed, Maya couldn't understand why other women waste so much time waiting for men to make the first move.

"When a guy isn't so worried about rejection," Maya says, "it just accelerates how often he reaches out to you."

Men are attracted to confidence, Maya says. Plus, men have so little experience with assertive women that the novelty itself becomes a huge turn-on.

> "I always tell my boyfriend what I want and what will make me happy in a relationship. He told me it's refreshing to be with someone who doesn't play games."

"It's like, 'This is different—let me see what this is all about,'" Maya says. "I always tell my boyfriend what I want and what will make me happy in a relationship. He told me it's refreshing to be with someone who doesn't play games."

Everything you've just read runs counter to what most women have been taught about men and dating. "If he does not approach, that probably means he's passive or a wimp," one Facebook friend tells me. "If the woman makes the first move, how does she know if he likes her enough?"

I know this woman, and I had to restrain myself from blurting out the first thought that popped into my head: "Wait, haven't you spent the last few years off-and-on-again dating a guy who you yourself told me thinks of you as a booty call? A guy who goes off camping with his buddies every weekend and who sponges off you financially? Did you ever think that maybe it's time for a different approach?"

Too many women have spent their entire adult lives convinced that men don't want women to ask them out, that men live for the chase, and that men will lose interest in you the moment you show too much interest in them. If this what you believe, your reaction to stories such as Evie's and Becca's may be to dismiss them as flukes.

Please don't. The latest research on men and dating illustrates how dramatically male viewpoints have shifted over the years. It shows why women like Evie and Becca succeed where others fail. A 2010 study out of the University of Copenhagen found that men are more likely than women to say yes when asked out on first dates.[8] Another study by behavioral scientist Shari Dworkin and social psychologist Lucia O'Sullivan found a wide gap between how men approach dating and what men actually prefer. In practice, men in the study were three times more likely than women to make the first move. But in preference, a majority of those same men wanted the women to make the first move. All in all, 72 percent of men reported a preference for women initiating, according to the study.

"Perceiving oneself as an object of desire has frequently been associated with the cultural constitution of femininity and vulnerability and has not previously been a central part of constructs of heterosexual masculinity," Dworkin and O'Sullivan write. "However, it appears that this is not the case in this sample of college-aged men. Men openly described a preference to be more of an object of desire specifically through female sexual initiation."[9]

Dworkin and O'Sullivan conducted their study back in 2005. A decade and a half later, men seem even more open to female advances. A 2017 survey of 5,500 American singles by Match.com found that 95 percent of men were pleased when a woman asked for his number, and 94 percent reacted positively when a woman called after a first date. Men were also overwhelmingly in favor of women initiating the first kiss (95 percent) and initiating sex for the first time (94 percent).

So much for the theory that men need the chase.

I can guess what some of you are thinking. "If I come on strong, won't the guy think I'm needy? Or, even worse, desperate?"

Personally, I've yet to meet the man who ended things with a woman he liked simply because she was too enthusiastic about him. So why, then, do so many women believe this myth? I've got two explanations. One is that women are simply ascribing to men feelings that are actually fairly universal for both sexes. How many women reading this have broken up with a guy after his behavior crossed the line from attentive to creepy? Lots, I'm sure.

Nobody likes pushy, weird, obsessive behavior, and this isn't limited to dating. I coach Little League baseball, for example, and one year I was paired with a co-coach who clearly thought we were going to be best buddies. He'd call me five or six times a day—sometimes with lineup ideas or sometimes just to shoot the breeze. The first week of the season, he called so often that my wife joked that she was getting jealous. I desperately wanted to break up with my co-coach—and he and I weren't even dating!

Don't be that guy when you're actually dating, and you'll be just fine.

Another reason the myth of the overeager girlfriend scaring off the guy is so pervasive is that it serves a useful purpose for those who promote it. Consider the research of Tracy Vaillancourt, a psychology professor at the University of Ottawa. As Vaillancourt explains to the *New York Times*, it is women, not men, who tend to police the dating behavior of other women.[10] In order to demonstrate this, she set up a psychology experiment in which forty-three pairs of college-aged women were invited into a psychology lab for what they were told was going to be a discussion about female friendship.[11] The discussion was a ruse. The actual experiment began when a research assistant entered the room looking for one of the professors.

The research assistant was chosen because she was quite attractive. Vaillancourt's study describes the assistant as the "sexy confederate" ("confederate" being academic lingo for an individual who appears to be a study participant or bystander but is actually part of the research team). When the sexy confederate entered the room dressed casually—wearing jeans and a loose-fitting T-shirt—the women participating in the study barely noticed the sexy confederate's appearance. But when she entered wearing a low-cut blouse and a tight skirt, 74 percent of the female participants behaved badly once the research assistant departed the room.

One of the women in the study suggested that the confederate was dressed to have sex with a professor.

Another complained that the young woman's "boobs were about to pop out."

"What the fuck is that?" opined a third.

The point of all this is not to show how mean women can be to other women. What Vaillancourt describes as "indirect aggression" (and others might call slut-shaming or simply mean-girl behavior) may be hurtful, but it's still preferable to how some men respond in comparable circumstances—with verbal threats or violence. For my purposes, the only thing important about indirect aggression is that it works. Indirect aggression is an incredibly effective way for women to stifle their romantic rivals, according to Vaillancourt. She found that girls who demonstrate high levels of indirect aggression toward other girls as adolescents tend to enjoy above-average levels of dating success into their twenties. Being a victim of indirect aggression has the opposite effect, significantly delaying when young women find their first boyfriends and become sexually active. Vaillancourt concludes that being a victim of indirect aggression "predicted being in a dating relationship one year later [than normal], even when controlling for age, prior dating history, peer-rated social status, and peer-rated physical attractiveness."

The lesson here? If you really like a guy, go get him. And please, please stop listening to your friends.

> ## Join the Conversation on the
> ## *Make Your Move* Blog at JonBirger.com
>
> Do you think it matters who says "I love you" first? If so, why?

4

DATE WHO YOU KNOW

My son Alex returned home from high school one day with a big complaint.

Alex had a free period after lunch, and he really enjoyed spending this hour reading his Kindle in the school library. On the day in question, Alex had just finished reading a mystery novel by his favorite author, and he was planning on downloading a new one after lunch. But once Alex got to the library, he discovered that the school Wi-Fi was down.

"I couldn't download another book because there was no Wi-Fi," Alex said. "It was so annoying—I had nothing to read."

"Umm, Alex, where were you again?" my wife replied.

"The library."

Long silence.

"Oh," he said, "I see where you're going with this."

Perhaps you can guess where I'm going with this?

In this chapter, I'm going to make the case that our collective device dependency—specifically, our creeping preference for online transaction over human interaction—is just as harmful to modern romance as it is to teenage common sense. (Sorry, Alex!) Most of us realize that the connections we make in the real world are deeper and more meaningful than those made in the virtual one. Nobody turns on a computer to find a best friend, for instance. Yet when it comes to finding a life partner, more and more singles are going online, even though most do not actually enjoy online dating.

A recent SurveyMonkey poll found that 59 percent of women and 55 percent of men have negative opinions of dating sites and apps.[1] Another recent poll, this one from the Pew Research Center, found that 71 percent of online daters believe it is "very common" for people to lie on dating-app profiles, and that 50 percent believe it is "very common" for fraudsters to set up fake profiles to ensnare singles in romance scams.[2] Confusing as it sounds, Millennial and Gen Z singles are becoming addicted to something they dislike and distrust. The end result is they're now as oblivious to dating opportunities in the real world as my son Alex was to reading opportunities in his school library.

I got my start as a financial journalist, and the title of this chapter is borrowed from one of my all-time-favorite investing books, *One Up on Wall Street* by Peter Lynch. A legendary mutual fund manager at Fidelity Investments, Lynch had a simple yet brilliant message to mom-and-pop investors: "Buy what you know."

Lynch argued that the best investments for individual investors are often the ones staring them in the face. He was writing in the late 1980s, a time when it had become trendy for small investors to chase after obscure computer stocks with products and balance sheets that were tricky even for Wall Street pros to understand. "Unless you work in some job that's related to computers," Lynch wrote, "what could you possibly know that thousands of other people don't know a lot better? [But] if you own a Goodyear tire store and suddenly after three years of sluggish sales you notice that you can't keep up with new orders, you've just received a strong signal that Goodyear may be on the rise."[3]

Lynch's point is that it's easier to make good investment decisions with companies you already know—or companies your friends already know (Lynch made a home-run investment in Hanes after a coworker raved to him about Hanes's new L'eggs pantyhose)—than it is with companies you're learning about from scratch. Well, the same holds true for dating. It's easier to connect romantically with people whom you already know (or your friends know) than with people who are complete strangers. Problem is, singles nowadays are so stuck in their smartphones, their tablets, and their laptops that they've become a lot like those investors Lynch wrote about—chasing dates with total strangers instead of pursuing relationships with neighbors, coworkers, friends, and friends-of-friends whom they already know, like, and are attracted to.

Now, don't get me wrong. I understand the appeal of online dating. It's easy. There's less risk of rejection. You can do it from your sofa. You don't have to go to a trendy bar and pretend you actually enjoy that new craft beer that tastes like pine cone. Best of all, dating apps allow you to do what you could never do at a singles bar—prescreen for height, income, religion, dog person or cat person, and everything else that you think is a must-have in a partner.

It sounds so great in theory, yet, as many of you have probably discovered, it is not an easy way to find lasting love. Searching for a life partner online is like searching for thoughtful conversation on Twitter—it's possible, yes, but you've got to wade through so much muck to find anything good. There's a reason why online relationships fail more quickly than offline ones—and why they're less likely to lead to marriage too. If you are marriage-minded and spending ninety minutes a day swiping and texting on a dating app, this is not an efficient use of your time.

Before I delve into online dating's drawbacks, let me state up front that I am not opposed to all forms of online dating. While I do believe—and while science shows—that old-fashioned dating is more likely to lead to lasting love, I recognize that dating apps work well for certain kinds of daters. Indeed, they can be true godsends for those singles who've always had trouble finding love in the offline world. Here are some examples:

Small-town singles. When I was a writer at *Fortune* magazine in the 2000s, my beat included agriculture, and that meant spending more time in rural Iowa, Illinois, and Minnesota than your typical city slicker. I learned a lot about farm life, and one of the big surprises was how much the population in corn country was shrinking even as the farm economy was booming.

Corn was seven dollars a bushel in 2007, up from two dollars just a couple years earlier, and that made for some very happy farmers. But it wasn't just the high crop prices making farmers richer. Corn and soybean farming had become more efficient and less labor-intensive over the years. The introduction of next-generation planters, combines, herbicides, pesticides, and seeds meant a farmer could farm twice as many acres as he could thirty years ago.

What does this have to do with dating? When farming becomes less labor-intensive, it means fewer people live in farm communities. When the farm-town population declines, the dating pool shrinks, and that can pose big challenges for local singles. It's not the grandmas and grandpas who move away to find work. It's the young people.

The pickings can be mighty slim for singles left behind. In Ringgold County, Iowa, for example, there were only twenty-four unmarried men and twenty-nine unmarried women between the ages of thirty and thirty-four in 2017, according to US Census Bureau data. I can almost guarantee you that most of those single men and women already know each other. If sparks haven't flown by now, they probably never will.

That's why a dating site like FarmersOnly.com can be so helpful. It allows rural singles to connect with people a few towns or a few counties away, people with similar values and lifestyles whom they never would have met otherwise. Yes, one hundred miles may sound like a long way to drive for a date—but what else do Iowa corn growers have to do in February?

Newcomers. Say you just moved to Austin, Texas. Austin is one of the best cities in America for young singles, but it's hard to have fun if you don't know anybody. You don't have a friend group. You don't know the singles scene. And it's too soon to date at work. (I'm an advocate for workplace dating—the ultimate "date who you know" and the focus of Chapter 6—but it's probably best not to dive into an office romance right after starting a new job.) For people who just moved to a new city, online dating can be a powerful tool. Not only is it likely your best shot at finding a boyfriend or girlfriend, but going on a lot of online dates can help build up your friend group too.

Pandemic daters. Online dating was the only dating for most singles during the worldwide COVID-19 pandemic, and I'm all in favor of making the best of a bad situation. Some experts even believe quarantine made online dating better. "With the coronavirus lockdowns, many of you now have more time," Helen Fisher, Match.com's chief scientist, writes in the *New York Times.* "You aren't dressing in the morning, commuting to work or meeting pals after office hours. Many of you have more time to talk. Moreover, you have something important to talk about. Chitchat and small talk have become far less relevant. Instead, during this pandemic, singles are likely to share far more meaningful thoughts of fear and hope—and get to know vital things about a potential partner fast."[4]

My view at the time was enjoy it while it lasted. Once stay-at-home orders were lifted, singles wouldn't have time for two-hour, midday video chats. And while some long-term relationships were surely born during quarantine, I'm not sure online dating actually improved. Reports abounded of dating-app users experiencing an uptick in online harassment. Plus, the intense connections some singles thought they were making over DMs and video chat disintegrated once these couples finally met face-to-face. Yvette, a dental hygienist in Boston, told me that the sweet guy she met on Hinge and bonded with over Face-Time drinks turned out to be much different in person once they decided to meet offline and date for real. "There was a lot of underlying personality stuff that didn't come across [in texts or video chats]," she says. "He turned out to be non-empathetic, judgmental, and just tremendously defensive—always a victim of his circumstances."

Singles with disabilities and chronic health problems. A couple of years ago, I got a LinkedIn invitation from the founder of the Gutsy dating app. I had never heard of Gutsy, so I googled it. Turns out that Gutsy is an app for singles with digestive health problems, such as Crohn's disease or irritable bowel syndrome. (Get it, *Gut*sy?)

Yeah, I chuckled too. But the more I thought about it, I wished my initial reaction hadn't been so juvenile. Most of us have been out on dates when we weren't feeling our best. Maybe we ate or drank the wrong thing and suddenly started feeling a little queasy. I have a distinct memory of going out on a first date when I thought I was over a stomach bug—only to spend twenty minutes in the men's room. Needless to say, there was no second date.

Well, imagine if this weren't just a funny story or a one-time embarrassment but a constant struggle. Imagine what first dates must be like for people with chronic stomach problems. Imagine how reluctant you might be to get attached to anyone, knowing that the inevitable "So I have to tell you something" conversation may scare him or her away. An app like Gutsy can go a long way toward solving this problem by allowing singles with digestive problems to connect with others who sympathize and understand.

Gutsy isn't the only dating app aimed at singles with disabilities or health issues. Lemonayde is another dating app for people with chronic health problems. (Think: When life gives you lemons, make . . .) Another app, Glimmer, is designed for singles with cognitive disabilities, such as autism or traumatic brain injuries. Deafs.com is a dating site for deaf people. CancerMatch.com and CancerSurvivorDating.com help cancer survivors find love.

"I think we can all agree that no one wants to hear the phrase 'sick people should just date sick people,'" Lemonayde founder Niko Geoffroy says in an interview. "The mission is to help make sure that you're comfortable with who you are, without feeling like you have to apologize for your condition, especially when it comes to dating."[5]

The value of dating sites like these is that they provide romantic on-ramps for people who, otherwise, might have given up on dating altogether.

Celibate singles. If you think telling a first date you've got irritable bowel syndrome sounds embarrassing, just imagine what the "I have to tell you something" conversation is like for men and women who are unable to have sexual intercourse.

"Who's going to sign up for that?" says Laura Brashier, a former hairdresser who gave up on dating after surviving a three-year battle with stage 4 cervical cancer.[6]

As Brashier explains to *Time* magazine, surgery, radiation, and chemotherapy saved her life, but they also left her with a new normal—one that made sexual intercourse impossible. Brashier still had sexual desires and still craved companionship, but she feared men would reject her once she shared her secret. So Brashier began searching for singles like her—people who crave love and intimacy but cannot have intercourse. Her quest led her to found RomanceOnly.com, a dating site specifically aimed at people who cannot have sex.

Niche dating apps and dating sites make dating easier and love more attainable for people who may have never found love otherwise. That's why I like them. The reason I'm less enthusiastic about mainstream dating apps is because I do not think they make dating easier or love more attainable for the majority of their users.

In order to grasp why, you first need to understand the business model of the online dating industry. It's no coincidence that Match, Zoosk, and other dating apps almost never tout the overall efficacy of online dating in their advertising. Bounty claims its paper towels are more absorbent, Chevrolet claims its cars are more reliable, and Verizon says its network is fastest—yet online dating apps never claim to get you married faster than old-fashioned dating.

Why not? Dating apps do not make their money off happily-ever-afters. Their business models revolve around growing their membership revenues by attracting and retaining more and more customers. Some apps like Tinder make money off advertising too, and advertising also relies on a growing audience. Every time a Match or Tinder member gets married and stops using the app, that means one fewer paying customer. It also means one fewer set of eyeballs that can be monetized for advertising. Is it any wonder then that the words *married* and *marriage* do not appear even once in the 2018 annual report of Match's parent company, Match Group?[7] (Match Group's brands include Match.com, Tinder, Hinge, OkCupid, and PlentyOfFish.)

A good business outcome for Match Group is one that has users spending more time—not less—on its apps. Match doesn't want to get you off the market. It wants to turn you into a lifelong shopper. The company admits as much in its shareholder reports, boasting that "successful experiences also drive repeat usage."[8] Translation: Start dating someone terrific on Match, and you'll keep returning to the site in order to find someone even more terrific.

> Dating apps do not make their money off happily-ever-afters . . . Every time a Match or Tinder member gets married and stops using the app, that means one fewer paying customer.

Given the inherent conflict between the financial goals of dating-app operators and the romantic goals of many dating-app users, it seems logical to question whether online relationships are actually built to last. Research says no.

Aditi Paul is a professor of communications studies at Pace University in New York. In 2014, Paul analyzed data from the most comprehensive independent dataset on online and offline dating—Stanford University's "How Couples Meet and Stay Together Survey," which tracks thousands of daters over the duration of their dating experiences and relationships. The Stanford dataset includes multiple groups, or "waves," of daters. In the first wave, Paul found that offline relationships lasted, on average, four times longer than online ones. Couples who met offline were also twice as likely to marry as couples who met through online dating. The offline marriages were more successful too: Only 2 percent of married couples who met offline ended up separated or divorced during the time period studied versus 8 percent of the married couples who met online.[9]

> Offline relationships lasted, on average, four times longer than online ones. Couples who met offline were also twice as likely to marry as couples who met through online dating.

A different analysis of the same dataset—this one authored by Michael J. Rosenfeld, the Stanford professor, and Ruben J. Thomas, a sociology professor at University of New Mexico—purports to show that breakup rates "are not much influenced" by how couples meet. But that conclusion seems to hinge on how one defines "not much." According to Rosenfeld and Thomas,

16 percent of the couples who met online broke up within one year—versus 10 percent who met through friends, 9 percent who met through family, 8 percent who met as neighbors, 6 percent who met as coworkers, and 1 percent who met at church.[10] (Disclosure: Surveys funded by the online dating industry paint a rosier picture.[11])

In Paul's study, the differences in success rates for offline and online couples were not identical for every wave in the Stanford dataset. The overall findings clearly demonstrated, however, that relationships formed online were less likely to succeed than those formed offline. "Online couples tended to break up more than their offline counterparts [and] had lower odds of getting married," according to Paul.

Why are online relationships less successful? I've been arguing for years that hetero singles are ill served by the filter functions on sites like Match and OkCupid. Consciously or subconsciously, users tend to check off boxes for an opposite-sex version of themselves. In doing so, they eliminate people with whom they'd probably click had they met at church, the beach, or some other real-world venue.

The single biggest driver of romantic attraction is what psychologists call "perceived similarity"—how much you think you have in common with a possible partner. According to Arthur Aron, a psychology professor at Stony Brook University and an expert on the subject, perceived similarity is very different from actual similarity.

"Thinking you're similar matters a lot," Aron tells me. "Actually being similar does not matter much at all."

If perceived similarity is subjective, that doesn't bode well for dating sites like OkCupid that try to match people via objective metrics. Indeed, in a since-deleted blog entry, OkCupid founder Christian Rudder revealed an experiment in which OkCupid intentionally misrepresented users' compatibility with one another. What OkCupid found is that couples who were misled to believe they were 90 percent compatible—but in fact met only 30 percent of each other's search criteria—were just as likely to hit it off as couples who were a genuine 90 percent match. "The mere myth of compatibility works just as well as the truth," Rudder said at the time.[12]

If online dating filters and algorithms don't actually help you find a better match, then how can online dating be a better way to date?

It isn't. People who first meet face-to-face are significantly more likely to report perceived similarity than those who meet online. A 2016 study led by Susan Sprecher, a professor of psychology and sociology at Illinois State University, paired up two hundred college students for "get acquainted" interactions designed to evaluate perceived similarity and other markers of interpersonal compatibility.[13] Half the initial interactions were online, while the other half were in person. Sprecher found that the pairs who engaged in face-to-face interactions first were 10 percent more likely to report perceived similarity than the pairs who met online. The face-to-face pairings were also 8 percent more likely to report liking the other person, 10 percent more likely to report enjoying the interaction, and 25 percent more likely to report feelings of closeness as compared to the pairs who met online.

These gaps reveal something fundamental about how the human brain is wired—namely that we need face-to-face interaction in order to communicate effectively. This was never more apparent than during the COVID-19 pandemic, as science writer Julia Sklar explained in an April 2020 *National Geographic* report on so-called "Zoom fatigue."

"During an in-person conversation, the brain focuses partly on the words being spoken, but it also derives additional meaning from . . . whether someone is facing you or slightly turned away, if they're fidgeting while you talk, or if they inhale quickly in preparation to interrupt," Sklar writes. "These cues help paint a holistic picture of what is being conveyed and what's expected in response from the listener. Since humans evolved as social animals, perceiving these cues comes naturally to most of us, takes little conscious effort to parse, and can lay the groundwork for emotional intimacy."[14]

Texting and video calls impair these ingrained abilities, according to Sklar: "If a person is framed only from the shoulders up, the possibility of viewing hand gestures or other body language is eliminated. If the video quality is poor, any hope of gleaning something from minute facial expressions is dashed."

Couples who do meet online can find one silver lining in the latest research. In Sprecher's study, when the online pairs did eventually meet face-to-face, it was possible for them to close the rapport gap between them and the pairs who originally met in person. The only catch, according to Sprecher, is that the transition from online to offline interaction must happen quickly. In

Sprecher's study, the pairs who first met online later met face-to-face on the very same day. Much further delays, Sprecher writes, may be "problematic in regard to relationship development . . . The longer individuals wait to meet a potential romantic partner in a face-to-face setting, the more likely they are to engage in idealization processes that risk expectancy violation upon meeting [face-to-face]."

In other words, the longer that online daters put off the first date, the more likely it is that the other person won't live up to his or her online persona. This is a problem without a good solution, since most online daters do not want to rush into first dates with strangers they've just met online. (Some don't want to meet them at all. Writing in the *Telegraph*, London journalist Miranda Levy explains how she found her "boyfriend" through online dating—but is in no rush to actually meet him.[15])

Women in particular have good reason to take their time before meeting men face-to-face. The online date-osphere is filled with fakes and fraudsters and much worse. Even if we accept that there are romantic advantages to moving quickly from online messaging to a face-to-face meeting, those advantages are completely offset by women's safety concerns and by the very real need to make sure that Robert the handsome forty-year-old hedge fund manager isn't actually Billy Bob the fifty-five-year-old ex-con.

Just ask Mia, a forty-nine-year-old divorcée and online dating veteran. Mia said many of the men she matched with online had fibbed about their age, profession, marital status, and relationship goals (that is, whether they were seeking a committed relationship or just a hookup). "All you know about them is their personal branding, and half the time it isn't even accurate," says Mia.

Whenever she went out on a first date with a man she'd met online, Mia found herself spending more time "trying to figure out all the holes in his story" than trying to figure out if she actually liked him.

"You don't have any friends in common, there's no real connection," she says of online dating. "So your instinct is to always play the doubter's game."

Mia knew that the doubter's game was not conducive to falling in like or in love, but she felt it was necessary in order to protect herself. A financial consultant in Washington, DC, Mia is now engaged to a man whom she met through a mutual friend. The way she approached her first date with now-fiancé Stephen was completely different from how she had been approaching her online dates. She was less wary, much more open to new possibilities, she tells me.

> Making an emotional connection with someone requires a leap of faith. It requires trust. And it's always going to be harder to make that leap with someone who is a complete stranger.

"It's more of a believer's game," she says of old-fashioned dating. "If [my friend] liked Stephen, I already knew he had to be a decent human being. I was just more inclined to find the positive."

Making an emotional connection with someone requires a leap of faith. It requires trust. And it's always going to be harder to make that leap with someone who is a complete stranger. A 2014 study found that couples who meet through friends or family are significantly more likely to marry than couples who meet online. Even if the couple doesn't actually know each other before the first date, the mere fact that they have friends in common makes it easier for sparks to fly. The study's findings are "a testament to the importance of these networks for introducing new partners, serving as sounding boards, and evaluating prospective matches," according to the study's authors, Sharon Sassler, a sociology professor at Cornell University, and Amanda Jayne Miller, chair of the sociology department at the University of Indianapolis. "Many of our respondents implied that meeting through friends, or having friends know their partner, made the relationship more acceptable, natural, or inevitable."[16]

This was certainly true in Mia's case. Heading into her first date with Stephen, Mia knew little about him beyond the fact that he was well-liked by their mutual friend. For her, that was enough. She didn't google Stephen to death the way she would normally do with her online dates. As Mia said, she was playing "the believer's game." She knew that her friend would never set her up with a man who was unkind or untrustworthy or whose values did not mesh with her own.

As it turned out, Stephen was not precisely what she was expecting. Before their first date, the only photo she had of Stephen was him on a paddleboard. From the photo, she just assumed that he was outdoorsy.

He was not. The photo was taken on Stephen's first and only time on a paddleboard. But that was okay, Mia says—even though it probably would not have been okay had she met Stephen online.

"He was a little more intellectual than I was expecting," she says. "But even with that cognitive dissonance, I just wanted to give him the benefit of the doubt. It was actually the closest thing to love at first sight I'd ever experienced.

"I guess it's an example of how the old-fashioned ways still work better!"

The old ways definitely work better if you're a true romantic. There's a reason why romance movies like *Serendipity*, *13 Going on 30*, *Notting Hill*, *When Harry Met Sally*, *Love & Basketball*, and *Definitely, Maybe* remain date-night favorites. There's also a reason why the rom-com genre will never include a film adaptation of *Data, a Love Story*—tech journalist Amy Webb's book all about how she reverse engineered her online dating profile in order to nab her optometrist husband. Even as singles spend ever more time in the virtual world, they still fantasize

> "It was actually the closest thing to love at first sight I'd ever experienced. I guess it's an example of how the old-fashioned ways still work better!"

about finding a soul mate in college, in the workplace, or even just by walking down the street.

It's not just women who harbor such fantasies. In an interview coinciding with the fifteen-year anniversary of the release of *Serendipity*, star Kate Beckinsale reveals that she is constantly surprised by how many men tell her that *Serendipity* is their favorite movie. (*Serendipity* tells the tale of two twentysomethings who meet while fighting over a pair of gloves at Bloomingdale's, fall in love over hot chocolate, and then—somewhat inexplicably— leave it to fate to decide whether they'll ever see each other again.)

"What's funny about that movie," Beckinsale tells *Bustle*, "is that if people come up to me in the street or at the store and say, 'My favorite movie is . . .' and they say *Serendipity*, nine times out of ten, it's a man. I find [it] really amazing considering I've done so many movies considered a 'guy' movie. I can pretty much predict if a guy is gonna come up to me to mention their favorite movie, it's always *Serendipity*.

"It's a hopeful sign that they like that movie so much. All the machine guns I've fired, the boys like *Serendipity* better!"[17]

Why are people so drawn to a film like *Serendipity*? It's not because these films are cinematic masterpieces (though I am a big fan of *Definitely, Maybe*—the best of the genre, in my opinion!). The reason these films resonate is because the stories of how we meet—and the levels of importance we attach to these stories—can actually foretell future happiness. Indeed, the entire plot of *Definitely, Maybe* revolves around a lonely, just-divorced Ryan Reynolds telling his ten-year-old daughter the story of how he and her mother, his ex-wife, first met—which leads him to a romantic epiphany about a lost love.

If two people connect on a dating app and prove compatible, you might think that the mundane, mechanical story of how they first met would not matter. But science shows that it can matter. A 2010 study in the journal *Memory* found that happy couples often share an unspoken agreement on the significance of the moment when they met. These "first encounter" memories can "anchor a couple's story and reflect the current and future hopes of a relationship," according to UC Santa Barbara psychologist Nicole Alea. "Vividly and emotionally remembering the first sight of love may function to sustain satisfaction in one's marriage."[18]

There's a reason some couples who meet on Tinder or other apps still fib about how they actually met. Sarah Sullivan and Sean Watson, a young couple in Toronto, told all their friends that Sean kept making up excuses to visit the bookstore where Sarah was employed and eventually worked up the courage to ask her out. In reality, they met on OkCupid. "We felt that our story is not remotely romantic," Sullivan tells the *Toronto Star*, explaining the lie.[19]

Television, film, and literature all accentuate the importance of "how-we-met" stories, according to Katherine Panattoni, a behavioral science researcher and lecturer at Aarhus University in Denmark. People tend to judge their romantic relationships through the lens of "master narratives of what relationship stories are supposed to look like," Panattoni tells the *Toronto Star*. It's partly why couples like Sullivan and Watson feel compelled to lie about their relationship origins.

Thing is, these master narratives exist for a reason. How-we-met stories serve as mortar for many successful relationships—a theory first advanced in 1980 by the late (and aptly named) psychologist and relationship scientist Dr. Philip Belove. Belove dubbed these stories "first encounters of the close kind"—a play on the title of the hit movie in theaters at the time. He argued that first-encounter memories capture the hopes of a marriage in a story, one that illustrates not just what the relationship was like but what it will always be like. On Belove's website, there's a truly beautiful example of why such stories can be so powerful.[20] (If you're a crier, beware. This one's a tearjerker.)

Belove's story began at a funeral—for the wife of a close friend. "She was beautiful and brilliant and a great mother and an athlete and light-hearted and friendly and dearly loved her husband and her life with him," Belove writes. "He was handsome, successful, good-hearted and very much in love with her. They were generous people. They had three children and adopted a fourth.

"It was a picture too good to be true, it seemed, and in her late forties when she went for her yearly check-up, they discovered a brain tumor."

At the funeral, the husband gave a eulogy that included the story of their own first encounter of a close kind. The husband, a doctor, was in the early years of his internship at a New England hospital. The work was challenging, the hours were long, and the days off few. Whenever he had time off, he would go on long hikes in the mountains to decompress.

"Specifically, there was one mountain and it took him all morning to get to the top and then all afternoon to get back down," Belove writes. "The view was, and is, spectacular. You could look east through several valleys to a distant city and beyond it, you could see the East Coast of New England and the Atlantic Ocean."

With little time for dating, the doctor sometimes used this climb as a handy screening device for possible girlfriends. On a first date, he'd mention his favorite hike in passing. If the woman indicated she couldn't make the climb or didn't want to, the doctor would know this was not a woman who could keep up with him. He'd know she was not a good match.

"He told us all this from the stage in the church at the funeral," Belove writes. "I seem to remember that the casket of his dear departed wife was behind him as he spoke.

"When he met the woman who would become his wife, they liked each other immediately," Belove continues. "He then told her about how he enjoyed hiking the mountain on his weekend off. He wondered how she'd respond. Would she be interested in joining him on the twelve-hour hike? Or would this be another addition to his reject pile? He told her about the beautiful view and the ocean in the distance.

"As if to compose himself, he paused his storytelling. She gave him an answer he wasn't expecting.

"'I have an idea,' she'd said, 'why don't we start the hike at midnight with flashlights? Then we'll be up top in time for the sunrise. We'll eat our breakfast there and then head back and we'll be back in time for dinner somewhere.'

"That was it," according to Belove. "The story said it all. It summarized their life together, how it was going to be and then how it was. Whatever he was up for, she'd be with him 150 percent.

"For him it was a glimpse of their destiny."

Not every couple will have a story so magical, of course. But even ordinary first meetings can still offer a little glimpse into the future. When I first met my wife in college, I certainly did not know that we'd eventually date or marry or raise a family together. But on some level I think I did sense that we were compatible.

Online daters don't have the same sort of how-we-met stories that can bind and explain who they are as a couple and why they are meant to be together. And that's probably one reason why some online couples still fib to friends and family about how they actually met. They make up stories about a knowing glance at a Christmas party or accidentally spilling coffee on each other at Starbucks. Why do they do this? Because their actual first encounters were filled with more anxiety than excitement. Can you imagine a woman on an online first date suggesting a midnight mountain climb to a man she'd just met on an app?

In her study, Sassler, the Cornell professor, notes how internet daters "often commented on their nervousness prior to meeting their partners for the first time, and a few indicated how they arranged to meet in 'safe' spaces." If that is your mindset going into a first date, it doesn't matter how well matched you are with the person across the table from you. A glimpse of a future together is not going to be on the menu.

If there is a connection between the story of how we meet and the story of what we may become, what does that say then about relationships that begin not with magical moments but with fact-checking and escape plans? How much harder is it for those relationships to succeed? Every relationship, every marriage, has its rough patches. Are people going to fight as hard to save a relationship formed over an algorithm and weeks of cautious texting as they would a relationship incubated on an early-morning hike capped off by a perfect sunrise? I think not.

> If there is a connection between the story of how we met and the story of what we may become, what does that say then about relationships that begin not with magical moments but with fact-checking and escape plans?

Rather than strengthen bonds, dating apps' free-market approach to romance has the opposite effect—"potentially suppress[ing] the desire for getting married," according to Paul's study.[21] The problem boils down to paradox of choice.[22] According to another study, this one authored by a pair of University of Wisconsin researchers, when online daters are given abundant options, they tend to be less satisfied with the partner they ultimately choose. Says Catalina Toma, a professor in the University of Wisconsin's Department of Communication Arts: "Sifting through choices is potentially problematic in that it can create the perception that the grass is always greener."[23]

Given lots of options, online daters struggle to choose. They are more prone to buyer's remorse once they finally do make a decision. A chance encounter at Bloomingdale's can be fate, your office crush moving to the cubicle next to yours can be destiny, but a careful evaluation of ten online suitors feels more like commerce. Every smart shopper knows their purchases can be returned, and online daters seem to be embracing a similar consumerist mindset. As Paul writes, "Individuals find it difficult to be locked into one particular dating partner when they know that hundreds of other potential dating partners are available."[24]

I visited with Paul at her Pace University office to discuss her research. In person, Paul seemed to choose her words more judiciously than in print. "I'm not going to say that all online dating is bad, or that all offline dating is good," she says. Not everybody uses a dating app to find a life partner, she reminds me. Some people just want to make new friends. Others are seeking out sex partners or non-monogamous romantic relationships.

Those are all excellent points. I agree with Professor Paul that there are good reasons to use dating apps that do not involve a quest for a spouse or a long-term partner. Happiness comes in many forms, and if you can find a friend with benefits using a dating app—or even a friend without benefits—that's great.

Thing is, if you purchased this book, you probably are not looking for a platonic friend or an occasional hookup. People who read dating books tend to be searching for life partners—and this shapes my negativity toward online dating. So for all the reasons stated above, I urge you to put down your phone and start exploring all the dating opportunities that exist in the real world.

How to begin? Read on . . .

Join the Conversation on the
***Make Your Move* Blog at JonBirger.com**

My favorite romantic comedy is *Definitely, Maybe* starring Ryan Reynolds and Isla Fisher. (I love the political-junkie backstory.) What is your favorite rom-com—and why?

5

THE *MAKE YOUR MOVE* OFFLINE DATING CHALLENGE

Welcome to the *Make Your Move* Offline Dating Challenge.

Consider it a romantic cleanse. It's sort of like a juice cleanse, except this one improves your love life instead of your immune system. Follow my advice for three months, use the blueprint below, and you can thank me later. Please post your experiences—the good and the bad—on the *Make Your Move* blog at my author website, JonBirger.com.

STEP ONE. Delete every dating app from your smartphone or tablet. Log out of every dating site on your laptop. Turn off all your notification emails. Remember, for any cleanse to work properly, you cannot cheat. You need to be all in.

STEP TWO. Make a list of all the single men in your life whom you've ever wondered about. Go through your immediate friend group, past and present coworkers, friends you've kept in touch with from college. That charming real estate agent who helped you find your last apartment. The cute cop you banter with at the deli. The trainer you know from your gym. The nice guy in apartment 5E who's always walking his golden retriever.

If you've ever wondered about dating him, he needs to be on your list.

STEP THREE. Now build your list by asking friends and family for help. I understand that this will not be easy. It's embarrassing to ask friends for setups. It's hard for them too. Nobody wants to offend a close friend by setting her up with a man who may not be up to her standards.

Please post your experiences— the good and the bad—on the Make Your Move blog at my author website, JonBirger.com.

I have two solutions to this problem. The first one is easy: Just blame me. Tell your sister-in-law or your best friend from college, "Hey, I'm reading this crazy dating book that wants me to do an 'online dating cleanse.' I already bought the book, so I figured what the hell. The author wants me to compile a list of potential offline dates—you know, how people used to meet before Tinder. He also wants me to reach out to friends and family and ask if you know any single guys you could set me up with. I know it sounds silly, but can you help?"

My second solution to the awkwardness problem—and this one comes courtesy of Mia from the last chapter—requires you to do a little homework. Let me explain. Odd as it may sound, one of Mia's long-standing dating "problems" is that she looks more like a 1950s movie star than the kind, generous, financial whiz she truly is. Her friends (myself included) have always been reluctant to set her up because we didn't know any men who were in Mia's league.

Mia came up with her own solution to this problem. It begins with pouring a glass of wine (or two—this may take a while). Next: Visit the Facebook pages of the husbands of your married friends and then scroll through the husbands' friend lists. "Specifically the husbands you admire," Mia says. She figures that if the friends' husbands are kind and smart and funny, there is a pretty good chance that the husbands' single friends might be all of those things too.

After identifying the prospects who seem most interesting, the final step is to talk to your friends about their husbands' friends. If the reviews you get back are positive, you then ask for a setup.

"This way they don't have to think as much because you've already done the legwork for them!" Mia says.

Now add the friends-and-family names to your original list. Maybe the new, combined list has three names on it. Maybe it has thirty. Everybody's list will be different. But once you're done compiling, I want you to consider how different this list is from the matches you've gotten from Match, OkCupid, or another dating app. I want you to compare your comfort level and interest level in these men to your matches online. I want you to ponder which dates are more likely to prove worthwhile.

Men on your offline list are real people—men whom you can probably trust to act like decent human beings on a first date. Your online matches? Who knows? London radio host Verity Geere probably speaks for a lot of women when, in an interview with the *Sun* newspaper, she sums up the men of online dating this way:

- the used-car salesman who told Geere that she "needed to lose a few pounds" moments before shoving his tongue down her throat
- the creep who asked Geere to "belch in his face" because it turned him on
- the homely American who used fake photos to trick Geere into a first date and then proceeded to offer her the keys to his apartment—so she "could go there to 'freshen up' and wait for him while he met some friends"
- the guy who dropped his trousers and suggested a "quickie" the moment Geere walked in the door of his house (Geere demurred—at least until after going to a party with him. "I did sleep with him that night," she admits, "but let's just say it wasn't memorable")
- the guy whom Geere met on Bumble and whom she thought was the one—but who ghosted her with no explanation after six months of dating ("I was devastated," she reports, "especially because I could see he'd

read my WhatsApp messages but didn't think enough of me to even reply")[1]

Zahra Barnes, writing for *Glamour*, has one more addition to the type-of-men-you-meet-while-online-dating list: the guy who acts totally different in person versus how he acted online. "Via text," Barnes writes, "his witty banter made your heart beat faster. But in person, he's like a cardboard cutout of the guy you thought you would meet—the same on the surface but stiff as a board when you try to get anything out of him. There's little as disappointing as a guy who gives good text but can't back it up in person."[2]

It could be the reason he can't back it up in person is that he wasn't the one giving you good text to start. Several years ago, I met entrepreneur Scott Valdez at a dating industry conference in Las Vegas. Founder of a company called VIDA Select, Valdez employs a team of modern-day Cyrano de Bergeracs who, for a fee, will take over clients' online dating accounts and then use their keyboard charms and banter skills to land them first dates with unsuspecting singles.

To be fair, Barnes and Geere met some decent guys online too. And yes, I realize that the "first date from hell" existed long before Al Gore invented the internet. But what makes online dating so much more prone to awfulness is the complete lack of accountability. Anybody who's spent ten seconds on Twitter understands that it's easier to behave badly when you're trading messages with strangers than it is when you're conversing face-to-face with people whom you actually know. The guy you know from church isn't going to ghost you. Your affable coworker probably isn't going to send you a text calling you a bitch. And your best friend's cousin understands there will be serious repercussions if he aggressively demands sex and then curses you out when you decline.

Consider the cheery ending to Geere's own story. She did her own version of the *Make Your Move* Offline Dating Challenge—she quit all dating for three months. Once her "detox" was over, she started dating a colleague from work.

They now live together.

"Our first date was at a local pub and I very quickly realized we had amazing chemistry," Geere says. "We laughed all night, and it felt so natural compared to the many awkward dates I'd put myself through. There had been no filtered photos, embellished profiles, or weeks of trying to impress one another with witty messages. He put me at ease and I didn't feel any of the cynicism that had previously weighed me down."[3]

The whole key to the Offline Dating Challenge is that these are men whom you already know or men whom your friends or family already know. You don't need to spend hours googling these guys just to make sure that they're not married, not axe murderers, and not seventy-five-year-old retirees posing as thirty-five-year-old heart surgeons.

The whole key to the Offline Dating Challenge is that these are men whom you already know or men whom your friends or family already know. You don't need to spend hours googling these guys just to make sure that they're not married, not axe murderers, and not seventy-five-year-old retirees posing as thirty-five-year-old heart surgeons. You won't need to spend weeks texting back and forth to make sure you're going to be comfortable meeting them face-to-face. As with Mia and her fiancé, Stephen, you'll probably be comfortable going out on a date with them as soon as you put them on your list.

STEP FOUR. Rank your list, starting with the men whom you would most like to date.

This will be a new experience for some of you. Up until now, dating has always involved men choosing you and then you evaluating whether those men who ask you out are worthy of your time. Doing the choosing will be something different.

Guys have lots of experience with this, so let me offer you some advice before you start ranking your list. A guy will often ask out the woman he thinks is most likely to say yes ahead of the one he actually likes best. He does this because it's easier on his ego. He does this because he, like you, fears rejection. Then years later, maybe he discovers that the woman of his dreams—the one he was always afraid to ask out—liked him too.

So my advice? Don't do what guys do. You've come too far to settle now. Please, please, please, do not rank your third choice ahead of your first just because you think third-choice guy is more likely to say yes if you ask him out on a date. If the guy who gives you the happiest happy feeling is someone from work—but you're worried he's just nice to everyone, and boy would it be awkward if that were true—he should still be number one on your list. You're not shopping for a used car here. You're searching for a life partner. A soul mate. I don't want you to wake up ten years from now and wonder about what might have been.

STEP FIVE. Ask your first-choice guy out on a date (and maybe your second choice too, assuming they don't know each other).

How you do the asking is important. Do not ask him in a wishy-washy, roundabout way. Do not ask your coworker if he wants to grab lunch sometime. He may just think you are being nice (which you probably are!).

Be specific. Don't be afraid to use the word *date*. Depending on how well you know the guy, you could even try out Becca's line: "Hey, are you ever going to ask for my number?"

Your instinct will be to create some wiggle room, some deniability, just in case he says no. But saving face should not be your primary concern. There should be zero uncertainty in his mind that you are asking him out on a real date. Again, you've come too far to have things go awry simply because you were not clear and he was as oblivious as all those guys on AskReddit.

Be direct: "Would you like to go out with me on Friday night?" Ask the question and wait for the answer. Let him fill the silence.

If he responds, "You mean, like on a date?" your response should be a simple and honest "Yes, a date" or "Yes, I hope that's okay."

If he asks why him, again keep it simple but truthful: "Because I like you?" Or, "I've always liked you—but if you don't feel the same, that's totally okay. We can still be friends."

There are three possible outcomes here.

Outcome one: He says no.

Believe it or not, this is not a terrible outcome. It may feel terrible in the moment. But if he says no, the good news is you'll never again have to wonder if he was the one.

That was Jenna's experience. I met Jenna three years ago at a dating event where I was speaking. Jenna asked me a question during the Q&A. The answer I gave her was way too snarky. I felt bad and sought her out afterward to apologize.

We got to talking, and Jenna wound up sharing her big dating dilemma. She had moved from LA to New York for an acting job, but there was a guy back in LA—Mike—whom she couldn't get off her mind. She and Mike had dated for a couple of months before she moved, which wasn't long enough for her to tell him how she really felt.

"I've dated other people since then, had sex with like four or five guys, and I still can't get over him," Jenna told me. "I just felt something different with him, and it's starting to drive me insane."

My recommendation to Jenna was to tell him what she had just told me and then see what happens. I asked her to let me know how it turns out.

She took my advice and texted Mike a few days later.

She got back the following reply: "Jenna, I started seeing someone here in LA which explains my distance. I should have told you sooner, but I really want to stay friends and on good terms."

Obviously, this was not the answer Jenna was hoping for. It stung. But Jenna was still glad that I had pushed her to open up to Mike.

"It's totally fine," Jenna said when I asked if she had any regrets about taking my advice. "I mean we do live three thousand miles apart. The big thing is at least now I have the answer."

At least she has the answer. That's the key. If this happens with a man on your list, just chalk it up to nothing ventured, nothing gained. Cross him off your list and move on to the next guy.

Outcome two: He says yes, is thrilled beyond belief, and tells you he's been trying to work up the courage to ask you on a date for months or years. This is the ideal outcome, obviously, and I suspect that many, many, many readers who participate in the *Make Your Move* Offline Dating Challenge will get exactly this response. (Again, please share your stories on the *Make Your Move* blog!)

When London-based relationship writer Dami "Oloni" Olonisakin asked her Twitter followers to "ask that guy you fancy out on a date and tweet me a screen shot of his response,"[4] she got back lots of stories of men who were thrilled beyond belief that their secret crush had asked them out:

> "Finally. I can't believe this is truly happening. Of course."

> "Yes yes yes."

> "Hell yeah!! I've been in love with you since the day we met."

> "Well damn. You just made my damn day. I've been trying to figure out how to ask you since the longest . . . You never stop amazing me. It's a date."

If this happens to you, congratulations. You can thank me by posting your story on the blog. (Or better yet, by buying *Make Your Move* for a friend!)

Outcome three: He says yes, but his yes is a little indifferent or reserved—for example, "Yeah, okay" or "Sure, where are we going?"

This one is tricky. The reason I want you to make it abundantly clear that you genuinely like him and are asking him out on a proper date is that the middle ground is too susceptible to misinterpretation. The more honest you are about your true feelings, the less likely it is he'll try to take advantage of you.

This probably sounds counterintuitive. But from a guy's perspective, a woman who coolly says, "Hey do you want to grab a drink with me after work on Friday?" is more likely to be looking for a hookup than the one who nervously asks, "Hey . . . so I know I'm going out on a limb here, but I've always liked you and I feel really comfortable around you . . . and I was wondering if you would like to go out on a date with me on Friday night?" His response to the former is more likely to be opportunistic, whereas his response to the latter is more likely to be sympathetic.

Psychologists call this "the beautiful mess effect." It turns out there's a sizable gap between how we interpret vulnerability in others and how we perceive vulnerability in ourselves. "Vulnerability is courage in you and inadequacy in me," writes Brené Brown, a professor at the University of Houston and the author of *Daring Greatly: How the Courage to Be Vulnerable Transforms the Way We Live, Love, Parent, and Lead.*[5]

No display of vulnerability evokes higher levels of admiration and affection than a confession of love, according to a study by a trio of psychologists at the University of Mannheim in Germany. "Falling in love, we are often afraid to speak openly about our feelings," the authors write. "Yet, if we stay silent, the thoughts about what could have been can haunt us for a long time, whereas talking openly about our emotions might become the foundation of a good relationship . . . Given the discussed positive consequences of showing vulnerability, [it might be] beneficial to try to overcome one's fears and to choose to see the beauty in the mess of vulnerable situations."[6]

So yes, his tepid acceptance of your date offer may mean he's not so into you. It could also mean he's just playing it cool. Either way, how you find out is not by playing it cool yourself. You need to make yourself more emotionally vulnerable, not less so. I'm not telling you to throw yourself at him. What I'm asking you to do is find out if your feelings about Mr. First Choice are reciprocated, and that means telling him truthfully why you asked him out in the first place.

Use the Offline Dating Challenge as part of your explanation, if need be. But just be honest with him, and see what happens. Maybe his answer will turn into your own first encounter of the close kind—the story the two of you tell your kids someday. If not, if he still seems ambivalent or if it's clear he was just hoping to get laid, then you've got your answer.

Remember, this is not a first date with a complete stranger. This is someone you already know. If he doesn't seem as enthusiastic about you as you are about him—especially after you so courageously put yourself out there—there's no need for a second date. Just cross him off your list and move on.

Again, please post your Offline Dating Challenge stories on the *Make Your Move* blog. I want to hear how your offline dates went. I want to hear how they compare to all the online dates you've been on. Other readers will want to hear about your experiences too, and they'll chime in with their own thoughts and stories. Not every offline date will be life changing, of course, but I truly believe many of you will find partners and soul mates who were right under your nose all along. And by sharing your stories with others, you'll inspire them to stop looking for love on their phones and tablets—and to start scrolling through the real-world men in their lives instead.

Join the Conversation on the *Make Your Move* Blog at JonBirger.com

How do your own worst online dates compare to Verity Geere's?

6

LONG LIVE THE OFFICE ROMANCE

For Bridget, a stroll down memory lane turned into a life-altering epiphany.

It was 1996, and Bridget had just gotten off the train in New Rochelle, New York—her hometown—to meet her dad and stepmom for brunch. Visits home had always been a little melancholy for Bridget. Bridget's mother died when she was only thirteen, and the pain of this loss always felt sharper when she was back in New Rochelle.

But this particular visit would prove different. A journalist in her late twenties, Bridget walked by the supermarket where her mom regularly took her grocery shopping. She passed the salon where she and her mom got facials. Her thoughts began to drift. Bridget started wondering whether she would ever get married and have children like her mom did.

"I wasn't sure up until that point," Bridget tells me, many years later. "I didn't know how I'd meet someone. I'm not the kind of person who goes out to bars or stuff like that."

It wasn't long before Bridget's daydreaming turned to the sort of man she hoped to marry someday.

Someone kind and funny.

Someone really smart.

Someone like Rob McDonnell, the guy in the cubicle next to hers at the New York City newspaper where she worked.

That guy who was always so nice to her. The one who kinda-sorta invited her to attend a coworker's wedding with him—but then got nervous when she pressed him on whether it would be a date.

"I was just wandering around, thinking about life, when suddenly it all came to me," Bridget says.

"I realized I did want to get married. I wanted to finish my mother's life, and . . . and . . . I wanted to marry Rob McDonnell!"

Rob and Bridget had worked together for almost a year. Their relationship was platonic, but they were definitely close. They worked late together. Ordered takeout together. Attended conferences. Trusted each other. Knew each other's quirks, their senses of humor, their pet peeves. Plus, their upbringings were remarkably similar—both raised by Irish American parents whose politics leaned liberal and whose demands for academic excellence were unrelenting.

Bridget's romantic epiphany came with one major compli-cation. Rob had just left New York City for a new assignment at their newspaper's Washington, DC, bureau. Still, Bridget decided to take a chance. She drafted a love letter, sent it to Rob, and then waited nervously to find out if he felt the same way about her as she did about him.

Unfortunately, Bridget didn't have Rob's correct mailing address, which led to a comedy of errors that would later become part of the punch line in Rob and Bridget's own meet-cute. The post office returned the letter to Bridget. Which led to an awkward phone conversation with Rob about getting his correct address. Which led to Rob asking Bridget why the heck she was sending him a letter in the first place.

"Why do you need my home address?" Rob said.

"Because I wrote you a letter, and I need to send it before I chicken out!" Bridget blurted.

And then she hung up.

I'm drinking tea with Rob and Bridget at their kitchen table as they tell me their story. Actually, they're retelling it to me. I've known Rob and Bridget as long as they've known each other—we all used to work together—but I'd forgotten many of the details of how they first began dating.

Rob and Bridget happen to be two of the most happily married people I know. They're good parents too. It's not always easy to predict which marriages will succeed and which will fail, but speaking as someone who knew Rob and Bridget way back when—back when they were "just friends"—I can tell you that this marital success story was easier to predict than Tom Brady's Patriots beating the Jets in Foxboro. Rob and Bridget were close friends before they began dating. They had weathered storms at work (including one literal storm when two huge windows blew out of our thirty-fourth-floor office). Everyone who knew Rob and Bridget knew that their marriage would work.

———

Why am I sharing Rob and Bridget's story? Because if you find someone who is a good partner at work, I believe there's a good chance he or she could be a good partner at home too (assuming you're attracted to each other, of course). In the previous two chapters, I made the case for dating people you know. Well, how many people do you know better than the people you work with? Not many, I'm guessing. This is why I believe the workplace is the single best place to find a romantic partner.

There are obvious caveats. Not all workplaces have a plentiful supply of the opposite sex, for example. A third-grade teacher won't meet many single men (or many men at all) in her elementary school's faculty lounge. A male aircraft mechanic will be similarly hard-pressed to find love in the maintenance hangar.

> The workplace is the single best place to find a romantic partner.

Even so, there's ample evidence that Cupid does love the workplace. A quarter of all office romances lead to marriage, according to Adrian Furnham, a professor of psychology at University College London.[1] Another study by CareerBuilder put the figure even higher, finding that 31 percent of office romances lead to marriage.[2] A third survey, this one commissioned to mark the season-eight DVD release of the romantic sitcom *How I Met Your Mother*, found that relationships conceived at work are more likely to result in marriage than those begun at a bar or on vacation or anywhere else. According to a spokesperson for the survey, "You might not think where you meet can affect how long a relationship lasts but it seems those who meet through work can expect more longevity than most."[3]

You don't need an advanced degree in relationship science to understand why the workplace is so conducive to finding a romantic match. People who work together already know each other, and their shared histories become building blocks for deeper connections. They have insights into each other's values, quirks, and priorities. They know what makes each other laugh. They know if there's chemistry between them before the first date. Perceived similarity—that thing so important to building successful relationships—has already been established. As Furnham puts it, "People with shared values have longer, happier relationships."[4]

> People who work together already know each other, and their shared histories become building blocks for deeper connections. They have insights into each other's values, quirks, and priorities. They know what makes each other laugh. They know if there's chemistry between them before the first date.

There's also a certain comfort level associated with dating at work simply because your coworkers have already been vetted. Stephanie Losee and Helaine Olen, authors of *Office Mate*, a book all about dating at work, liken a company's human resources department to a free matchmaking service. HR staff members have already checked references. They've verified education and employment history (which means you don't have to cyberstalk him to make sure he actually has an MBA from Harvard or really did spend five years in the air force). "They might actually find out if he *is* an axe-murderer," Losee and Olen quip.[5]

Assuming your HR department did its job properly, not only are coworkers unlikely to be axe murderers, but they probably won't be deadbeats either. According to a survey by HR.com and the National Association of Professional Background Screeners, 95 percent of employers perform not only criminal background checks on prospective hires but credit checks too.[6] The very best employers take the screening process even further. In addition to looking for smarts and ambition, they place a premium on conscientiousness and emotional intelligence. Many of the traits we value most in our romantic partners are the same ones HR departments value when assembling teams at work.

Another huge advantage to dating coworkers is you already know how they deal with setbacks and disappointments. Few things come closer to replicating a marital stress test than spending forty hours (or more) a week with someone as a coworker. Interacting with colleagues from nine to five reveals so much more about character than trading carefully worded text messages on an app or having an awkward first date over sushi. Online dating makes it way too easy to mask flaws. In the workplace, your values and personality traits are constantly on display. A man who is selfish and dishonest at work is going to be selfish and dishonest in a relationship too.

Dan and Mina met in an especially stressful workplace—the obstetrics unit of a major New York City hospital. Dan was a chief resident, and Mina was a medical student assigned to his eight-person team. Character gets revealed quickly in life-or-death situations.

Dan wasn't the first doctor at the hospital to ask Mina out on a date. Shortly before they met, she said no to another potential suitor. "He was handsome and nice and everything," Mina recalls, "but then he was like, 'Let's go drinking.' I was like, 'Wait, we're on call.'

"Any doctor who was going to drink while they're on call is not someone I'd want to have a relationship with. It's an ethical boundary I just wouldn't cross."

Dan, on the other hand, was an ideal role model for aspiring doctors. He had a nice way with expectant mothers and fathers. He never dumped scut work on medical students or other doctors. Nor did he treat nurses like second-class citizens (as other doctors sometimes did).

"I don't think I saw him yell at someone once," Mina says.

Plus, Dan was always making her laugh—and vice versa.

"Some of the things we were dealing with were so stressful, so sad, that it required a certain gallows humor," Dan explains. "If you didn't laugh, you'd cry."

Dan and Mina's first date was on the last day of Mina's obstetrics rotation. Twenty-five years later, they're still happily married, holding hands as they tell me their story.

"Once we started dating," Dan says, "it was all so easy."

"Easy peasy," adds Mina.

Dan and Mina knew immediately that they'd found their match. They didn't need a half-dozen dates to feel a connection. They knew everything important about each other before the first kiss. And that, in a nutshell, is what makes the workplace the perfect place to find a life partner.

Just consider how many of our favorite celebrity couples met at work: Barack and Michelle Obama. Bill and Melinda Gates. Beyoncé and Jay-Z. Many of our most beloved fictional couples started out as coworkers too: Meredith and Derek on *Grey's Anatomy*, Sam and Diane on *Cheers*, Mac and Will on *The Newsroom*, April and Andy on *Parks and Rec*, and (my personal favorite) Jim and Pam on *The Office*. Jim and Pam's entire relationship was built around the workplace. Had Jim and Pam met on Tinder, it probably would have been the most boring first date ever.

With so many great examples of couples who met at work and so much evidence to support workplace dating, office romances should be soaring in popularity. But they aren't. According to Rosenfeld, the Stanford University sociologist, the percentage of heterosexual couples who meet at work has dipped from 20 percent in 1990 to 10 percent in 2010.[7] This decline is even more surprising when you consider the level of gender balance in today's workplace versus the level thirty years ago. More women in the workforce should be translating to more potential couples, but that's not what's happening.

The rise of online dating is partly to blame for workplace dating's loss of luster. But the biggest problem is not so much competition from dating apps as cultural shifts in how the office romance is perceived. Well-placed concerns about sexual harassment—concerns that existed before #MeToo but are now top-of-mind for many employers—have tempered everyone's enthusiasm for workplace dating.

Several years ago, one of my *Date-onomics* readers—a young woman I'll call Emma—sent me a Facebook message asking for advice on how to deal with a "creepy coworker" who had asked her out on a date. Based on her description of the guy, he didn't sound like much of a catch. He was definitely lacking in social graces. But these were the early days of #MeToo, and Emma's biggest complaint was not the guy's dateability (or lack thereof) but the fact that a coworker had asked her out on a date at all.

On a lark, I asked Emma how her parents had met. (Actually, it wasn't a total lark—I had a vague recollection of Emma posting something about her parents on Facebook.)

Emma took a few minutes to reply.

"Okay, yes, my mom was a secretary and my dad was one of the young executives she did secretarial work for," she said. "He asked her out his second day on the job—so, yeah, I guess these days he might be considered the creep.

"But they've been together for thirty-four years!"

Quite inadvertently, Emma had stumbled onto the giant conundrum of workplace dating. The workplace is an ideal place to find a long-term partner—as Emma's own parents can attest to!—but it's also the trickiest one to navigate. If a guy asks out a girl from spin class, SoulCycle is not going to cancel his membership. But nowadays everyone from lawsuit-wary employers[8] to sick-of-being-objectified #MeToo advocates wants to put an end to coworkers dating other coworkers. As feminist writer Jaclyn Friedman tells CNN, "My fervent hope is that #MeToo will scare men into finally paying attention to women as people [and] realizing that they probably don't want to be hit on at work."[9]

Forty-three percent of Americans now want to prohibit any office romance that involves people at different levels, according to a survey conducted by the career site Vault, and lots of companies have adopted such policies.[10] Fashion designer American Apparel prohibits managers and subordinates from engaging in either "casual dating" or "committed relationships."[11] So too does McDonald's—and in November 2019 the fast-food king fired its unmarried CEO, Steve Easterbrook, for having a consensual relationship with another employee.[12] This sort of blanket ban would have kept apart some very high-profile couples, including Barack and Michelle Obama (she was his supervisor at the law firm where they worked), Bill and Melinda Gates (everybody at Microsoft was subordinate to Bill), and Tina Brown and Harold Evans (Brown worked for the *Sunday Times* of London when Evans was the editor).

There has got to be a way to allow these sorts of relationships to flourish while also stamping out the abuses. Facebook and Google may have hit upon the solution. In 2018, both tech giants implemented corporate fraternization policies that allow employees to ask a coworker out on a date once—but only once. If the coworker says no, the asker doesn't get to ask again. If he or she does, they're fired.

It's a sensible compromise. Office romances are still allowed to blossom, but the ask-once-but-only-once proviso tamps down on unwanted advances and harassment. Good ideas tend to get copied, and I expect this one will get copied by lots of other companies.

But what's good for employers and employees spells trouble for single women stuck in the 1980s when it comes to dating strategy. The new rules of workplace dating are incompatible with the rules of *The Rules* and all the other play-hard-to-get dating bibles. If you ask out a coworker at Facebook, any ambiguous reply such as "I'm busy" or "I can't that night" still counts as a "no," according to Heidi Swartz, Facebook's global head of employment law.[13] In other words, it's actually against the rules for guys to assume you're playing hard to get. The type of persistence that books such as *The Rules* demand from men is exactly the sort of behavior that will get those men fired.

Consider the story of Bill and Melinda Gates. According to an interview Melinda Gates gave to the AOL *Makers* podcast, Bill first asked her out in 1987—a few months after she was hired as a Microsoft product manager.[14]

"He said, 'You know I was thinking maybe we could go out, if you give me your phone number, maybe two weeks from tonight,'" Melinda recalls.

Melinda did what any self-respecting 1980s woman would have done—she played hard to get.

"I said to him, 'Two weeks from tonight? I have no idea what I'm doing two weeks from tonight.' And I said, 'You're not spontaneous enough for me.'"

Bill, however, would not take no for an answer.

"It was really sweet," Melinda recalls. "He called an hour later and said, 'Is this spontaneous enough for you?'"

The same story that may have seemed sweet thirty years ago would raise all sorts of red flags today. Melinda said no when the CEO of her company asked her out on a date. Bill still called Melinda back an hour later to ask again. How many Microsoft employees would have been 100 percent comfortable saying no twice to a date with their CEO? Had Bill Gates been CEO of Google in 2020 instead of CEO of Microsoft in 1987, Bill and Melinda's love story might have had a very different ending—a date for Bill with his general counsel.

The story of Melinda playing hard to get with Bill worked out in the end. But for every story like Bill and Melinda's, I bet there were three or four other Microsoft women who were not playing hard to get when they said no to bosses or coworkers who asked them out on dates. When men fail to take a hint, the work environment can become uncomfortable or hostile for women very quickly.

The good news is that men seem to be learning, slowly but surely. More of us realize that what might have been okay in 1987 is not okay in 2021. But if single women do choose to date at work—and like I said, I think it's advantageous—they too must adapt. Bill Gates doesn't strike me as a stalker or a creep.

Had he and Melinda met today—and had she responded today the way she did back then—my guess is that she would still be Melinda Ann French and not Melinda Gates. Bill would have interpreted Melinda's "You're not spontaneous enough for me" as a hard no and then set his romantic sights elsewhere.

So here's my advice to single women interested in dating at work:

1. If your workplace boasts a diverse group of singles, use it to your advantage. Yes, dating at work is complicated. But like I said, the office is the single best place to meet a life partner.
2. Be like Bridget and make the first move. The guy you like may be afraid to.
3. Don't be like Melinda. Just say yes if the guy you really like asks you out. Don't play games. There may not be a second chance.
4. Don't be like Bill. If you ask a guy out for drinks and he says, "Some other time," just take it as a no and move on. Anything else might get you fired!

Join the Conversation on the
Make Your Move Blog at JonBirger.com

What's your reaction to Melinda Gates's story of how Bill first asked her out on a date? Do you think Bill and Melinda's meet-cute would still be cute today?

7

GET 'EM WHILE YOU'RE YOUNG—OR THEY ARE!

There's a story I hear over and over from thirtysomething single women. Goes something like this:

I wasn't even looking for a husband in my twenties. My mom, my dad, my mentor at work—they all told me that my career should take priority and that having a man in my life would just distract me from my goals. I thought having it all meant having it all on my own timetable. No way was I going to deviate from my plan: Vice president by thirty. Married by thirty-two. Baby by thirty-five.

Plans such as these sound so perfect on paper. If women just wait till thirty to get serious about dating, not only will they be more emotionally and financially prepared for marriage, but their men will be more ready too. These women just didn't account for the man deficit. Too many of the men they thought they might marry were already off the market by the time they turned thirty.

"It feels like everyone else is just passing me by," an on-the-verge-of-tears thirtysomething named Alexandra told me a few years ago following a speech I gave at South by Southwest in Austin, Texas.

Alexandra's ex-boyfriend from college—a guy she thought she might end up with—had just gotten engaged. She was feeling envious of married girlfriends, the same ones whom she used to criticize for prioritizing baby over briefcase. She was shocked at how deftly some of these women were balancing careers and families, doing so in ways she once thought impossible.

Said Alexandra, "I'm now worried that my plan was wrong."

Had Alexandra been a little younger, I would have urged her to go read Meg Jay's book *The Defining Decade*. A psychologist with a stable of twentysomething patients, Jay's book is a plea to young people to stop postponing adulthood. Jay recounts a session with a young woman who rationalized her train wreck of a personal life by proclaiming that "thirty is the new twenty." Jay's retort in *The Defining Decade* is that thirty is not the new twenty. Thirty is still thirty. Our twenties are actually the most formative years of our adult lives, and they mustn't be wasted.

"Many twentysomethings assume life will come together quickly after thirty, and maybe it will," Jay writes. "But it is still going to be a different life. We imagine that if nothing happens in our twenties then everything is still possible in our thirties. We think that by avoiding decisions now, we keep all of our options open for later—but not making choices is a choice all the same."[1]

The reason so many single women feel overwhelmed in their thirties, Jay writes, is because they didn't make enough big decisions in their twenties—where to live, whom to marry, when to have kids, which career to pursue, and so on. They've discovered it's nearly impossible to answer these questions all at once because the answer to one question may not be compatible with the answer to another.

"Life does not end at thirty, but it does have a categorically different feel," according to Jay. "A spotty résumé that used to reflect twentysomething freedom suddenly seems suspect and embarrassing. A good first date leads not so much to romantic fantasies about 'The One' as to calculations about the soonest possible time marriage and a baby might happen."[2]

The reason I didn't suggest *The Defining Decade* to Alexandra is because Jay's book doesn't offer a whole lot of advice or solace to over-thirty women. Jay's message is squarely aimed at twentysomethings. She's imploring them not to make the same mistakes that their aunts or older sisters may have already made. Jay's book wouldn't have solved Alexandra's problems. It would have confirmed her worst fears.

I do have advice for Alexandra and other older singles on how to get back on track romantically. The second half of this chapter and both chapters that follow are squarely aimed at women like Alexandra. But before I offer up thoughts on how thirtysomething and fortysomething women can beat the rough dating odds and not be haunted by miscalculations of youth, I first want to address readers still in their twenties. I want to build upon Jay's warnings and explain why young, hetero, marriage-minded women should not put off getting serious about dating until their thirties. If you do, you should at least be aware of the risks.

Here's what you should know.

The Dating Market Gets Statistically Worse the Longer You Remain Single

Lopsided sex ratios won't matter to hetero women who do not prioritize marriage or monogamy. And they definitely don't affect same-sex daters. But if you're a hetero, college-educated woman who does put a high priority on marriage and who wishes to be with a similarly educated man, you need to know that your dating market will get statistically worse over time. This is something Alexandra discovered the hard way.

Educated singles who are now in their early twenties graduated into a dating market with one-third more women than men. Sex ratios are even more lopsided than that in some big cities. According to 2017 US Census Bureau data, Miami has 56 percent more women than men among college grads twenty-four and under; Los Angeles, 63 percent more women than men; and Washington, DC, 53 percent.[3] And in case you're wondering, no, you cannot move to Toronto or London in order to escape the man deficit. That's because the man deficit is not a uniquely American phenomenon. There are one-third more college-grad women than men in other developed countries too, including Argentina, Australia, Belgium, Brazil, Canada, Denmark, France, Israel, Lebanon, New Zealand, Sweden, Thailand, and the United Kingdom.[4]

As bad as the dating demographics start out for women, the imbalance tends to get worse the longer they remain single. A good way to visualize this is by imagining dating as a game of musical chairs. If you ever played musical chairs as a child, you probably remember that the odds of losing increase the longer you remain in the game. When there are twenty-five players and twenty-four chairs, your chances of losing are low—4 percent to be precise. By the last round, however—when there are only two players and one chair—your chances of losing soar to 50 percent.

Well, dating in a man-deficit world is a lot like playing musical chairs. Picture a dating pool that starts out with forty women and thirty men (which, thanks to assortative mating, is essentially the dating pool now confronting college-educated Millennial and Gen Z women). Once half the women get married—once twenty of the women marry twenty of the men—the dating pool among the remaining singles shrinks to twenty women and ten men. That's a 2:1 ratio. Once five more marry, the pool becomes fifteen women and five men, a 3:1 ratio. A dating market that started out with a 4:3 ratio of women to men becomes 2:1 and then 3:1 over time. If you've ever wondered why there are so many fabulous women in their thirties and forties who can't find a guy, this is why. The longer a woman puts off getting serious about dating, the greater her risk of not finding the right match.

It's unfair as hell. But unfortunately that's the world we live in.

No, You Don't Have to Put Your Career or Grad School on the Back Burner Just So You Can Find a Guy Before Turning Thirty

Young women today are bombarded with messages warning them that career and education must take precedence over finding love. It's too hard, they're told, to succeed professionally and financially if you've got a husband or serious boyfriend distracting you from what's truly important.

"Early twenties is essential for establishing yourself professionally whereas relationships could be formed at any time," advises Ellen Nguyen, a relationship writer based in London.[5]

"When you're single," adds Beca Grimm, a lifestyle columnist writing for *Bustle*, "you get to work when you want, all you want!"[6]

Perhaps you are someone who puts a far higher priority on building your startup or saving lives in the ER or teaching the next generation of cellists than you do on getting married. If so, I applaud you. Follow your passion. My warnings are not intended for you. Getting married and having children are not required in order to lead a happy and fulfilled life.

Thing is, if you do prioritize marriage, I urge you to live your life that way. And that includes questioning those who keep telling you that it's easier to excel in law school or get a raise at work if you're single. You've been told that relationships are a hindrance to financial and professional success. But what evidence is there that this is actually true?

A Cornell University study found that married, female graduate students completed their degrees faster than single peers and were also more likely to get their research published.[7] (The study used a dataset compiled by the Andrew W. Mellon Foundation and tracked 11,000 US graduate students over a twenty-year period.)

The corporate world is equally friendly to married women. It's well-known that marriage is good for men's wages, but new research reveals that there's a wage premium for married women too. A 2013 study by Harvard University sociologist Alexandra Killewald found that married women outearn their single peers by 3.7 percent, controlling for variables such as age, children, education, geography, job characteristics, and job tenure.[8] One possible explanation for the marriage premium is that married workers are more focused on maximizing their pay. Another is that employers discriminate in favor of married workers, believing married workers to be more reliable and less likely to job-hop. Yet another explanation (and this happens to be my own theory) is that people in long-term relationships have more time, not less, to focus on their careers.

The Harvard study isn't all good news for married women. A significant motherhood penalty still exists in the wage data, though it applies equally to all moms regardless of relationship status. (Remember, 40 percent of babies are now born to unmarried women in the United States, a figure that is even higher in European countries such as Denmark, France, Spain, Sweden, and the United Kingdom.[9]) Another negative for married women: Their marriage premium is still only half the 7.3 percent enjoyed by married men.[10]

Nevertheless, Killewald's research goes a long way toward debunking the idea that coupledom is inherently harmful to women's careers. Indeed, the women in Killewald's study didn't even have to be married in order to reap the financial rewards associated with being in a serious relationship. Killewald and her co-researcher found that unmarried women living with a partner outearned single peers by essentially the same amount—3.6 percent—as did the married women.[11]

The wage premium isn't the only financial advantage associated with coupledom. According to the *Atlantic*, women who are single spend, on average, $1 million more over their lifetimes on health care, housing, taxes, and other expenses than their married counterparts do.[12] That's a huge sum of money for anyone, but especially for young people saddled with $50,000 or more in college debt. Some of this is related to tax benefits associated with being married. Some of it is lifestyle (single people eat out more, travel more, spend more on apparel and beauty products, and so on). And some of it is simple economies of scale: Single women spend 40 percent of their income on housing, for example, whereas coupled women spend only 24 percent.

Finally, if it were true that women who stay single longer have better careers, you'd think that the most successful women in corporate America would be ones who married later in life. But that's just not the case. The top five women on *Fortune* magazine's

2019 "Most Powerful Women" list all got married in their twenties, and four of the five met their husbands before they turned twenty-three.[13] Marillyn Hewson, the CEO of Lockheed Martin and number one on the *Fortune* list, met her husband, James, in college. Mary Barra, CEO of General Motors and number two on the list, met her husband, Tony, in college too. Abigail Johnson, *Fortune*'s number three and CEO of Fidelity Investments, was twenty-six and a student at Harvard Business School when she got engaged to her husband, Christopher. Ginni Rometty, *Fortune*'s number four and the CEO of IBM, was twenty-two when she met her husband, Mark, who was a fellow management trainee at GM. Gail Boudreaux, CEO of Anthem and *Fortune*'s number five, met her husband in high school—and married him right after wrapping up her legendary college basketball career at Dartmouth College.

> "Career-wise, we both feel like we're at a serious and perhaps unfair advantage over our single friends. It's so important not having to worry about this one important part of your life at a time when so many other things in your life are still up in the air."

I'm not saying you have to marry young in order to be successful. But if the most successful women in corporate America were all happily coupled in their twenties, can we at least agree that you don't have to remain single in order to get ahead?

Liz, a thirty-one-year-old financial executive in Chicago, has been with her husband, Eric, since college, so she can't say for sure how her experiences in business school or the workplace might have been different had she been single. But she and Eric, a tech entrepreneur, are both absolutely convinced that being married has been a boon to both of their careers.

"We talk about this a lot," says Liz. "Career-wise, we both feel like we're at a serious and perhaps unfair advantage over our single friends. It's so important not having to worry about this one important part of your life at a time when so many other things in your life are still up in the air."

(Somewhere, Meg Jay is smiling.)

"I also feel like we're each other's best board of advisers," she continues. "I know everything about his job and his career and what he's thinking. And he knows everything about mine. You're going through it with someone who not only knows what you're going through but is invested in your success as well."

Being Single Is a Huge Time Commitment

Liz mentions "all the time we don't have to spend dating" as yet another reason why marriage has been good for her career. It's a great point. According to *Bustle*, Millennials spend ten hours a week on dating apps[14]—and that doesn't even include time spent on actual dates.

Ramona, a fifty-one-year-old screenwriter in Hollywood, agrees wholeheartedly with Liz's point about the single life being an enormous time suck. Ramona married her husband, Kevin—a musician turned college professor—back when she was twenty-two and he was twenty-five. As a young person trying to make it in Hollywood, Ramona discovered early on that being married gave her more time, not less, to advance her career. The single life was incredibly time-consuming for her single friends, she says. Just getting ready for dates seemed to be a two-hour time commitment.

Kevin worked long hours too, which meant that neither he nor Ramona had to worry that they were missing out on meeting potential dates just because they were still in the office at 8 PM rather than enjoying the singles scene at some trendy LA night spot. "There was a period when he was in grad school and he was busy all the time," says Ramona. "And there was a period when I was working on [a popular TV show], and I was the one who was busy all the time. But we were both fine with that. We supported each other.

"And we never had to worry about who we were going to go on vacation with!"

Marriage Is Always a Leap of Faith, and Those Leaps Get a Little Harder with Age

Ramona is thankful she never had to date in her thirties or forties. The expectations are too high, she says. The singles she knows in their thirties and forties all seem to have long lists of must-haves for potential partners. The right height, the right job, the right income. Must love to dance. Can't like to golf. "Oh," she adds, "and they have to be soul mates too!

"It's like their first dates are more like job interviews. It's like they're looking for hard evidence, but that's not how this stuff works."

The older we get, the choosier we become about our romantic partners. Two studies out of Australia found that once we become accustomed to a certain lifestyle, the pool of compatible singles shrinks significantly. Older men, for example, get much pickier about women's education level, according to Stephen Whyte, a behavioral economist at Queensland University of Technology.[15] Women find it harder to compromise too, according to a study by Rachel Thorpe, a research fellow at Australia's La Trobe University. The older, single women whom Thorpe surveyed "would have entered a relationship if the 'right' person were available," but they were generally "unwilling to compromise on relationship standards." As one interview subject tells Thorpe: "If I had a partner now, it would be somebody who had the wisdom of life and who is canny about the world, who is experienced and had philosophies that trained that experience."[16]

> Compatibility is not an exact science. The younger we are, the easier it is to accept the reality that we don't always know exactly who will make us happy.

I have no idea what that means, but I suspect such men are very few and far between.

Compatibility is not an exact science. The younger we are, the easier it is to accept the reality that we don't always know exactly who will make us happy. In Ramona's case, she got married thinking Kevin would be her first husband, not her only one.

"I never believed in the fairy tale," says Ramona. "I married Kevin because he was nice to me and he was fun, and back then we both liked to party. We were lucky that we were young and stupid."

Would they have made that same leap had they been older and wiser?

"I'm not sure," she says. "What I do know is that we had to learn how to adult together. As you know, marriage involves compromise, and once you hit your thirties or forties, I think it becomes harder to compromise because you're so used to living a certain way.

"I'm not saying it's impossible. I just think it's easier to grow together with another person when you start out younger."

Delaying Until Your Mid- or Late Thirties Carries Significant Reproductive Risks for Any Woman Who Wants Kids

Most women already know this, of course. But a few years ago I was on a panel with Dr. Lynn Westphal, a leading fertility doctor at Stanford University Medical Center. Westphal mentioned that she's always amazed by how many otherwise-intelligent people show up in her office believing modern medicine now makes it easy for women to have children in their forties and fifties.

"They've seen all these stories about famous actresses giving birth at age fifty," Westphal says.

It's not easy at all. The reality is that the odds of getting pregnant decline precipitously between ages thirty and forty. Egg freezing and IVF are not surefire solutions, especially when the woman's eggs have been harvested after age thirty-five. My friend Lisa Schuman, founder of the Center for Family Building, is a clinical social worker who works with families dealing with infertility issues.[17] Schuman told me it's heartbreaking how many women wind up in her office, despondent over their inability to conceive in their thirties or forties.

Says Schuman, "They spent their twenties trying not to get pregnant, and now that they're in their thirties or forties, getting pregnant is the most important thing in their lives."

———

So that's my pitch to twentysomething women about why they should not put off finding a partner until their thirties. But what about my advice for older women? What about the thirty-three-year-old who could have gotten married when she was twenty-seven and is now worried all the good men her age are taken?

My first suggestion: Stop dating men your own age and go back to dating twenty-seven-year-olds. Dating younger always worked for successful men. Shouldn't dating younger work for successful women too? My answer is yes—and humor me while I offer a roundabout explanation for how and why . . .

———

Celebrity news is not my thing. I don't watch the Grammys. I've never read *Us* magazine, and I definitely don't read TMZ.

My version of "new music" is Pearl Jam. So if you want to have a conversation about the rapper who's dating the reality star, I am definitely not your guy. But there is one category of celebrity news that has always intrigued me, and that is anything related to December-May romances. Whether it's fifty-two-year-old George Clooney marrying thirty-five-year-old Amal Alamuddin, forty-two-year-old Demi Moore marrying twenty-seven-year-old Ashton Kutcher, or sixty-five-year-old Dennis Quaid getting engaged to twenty-six-year-old Laura Savoie, these stories never escape my attention.

The reason for this is simple. My father is ninety-seven; my mother is eighty-seven. I'm writing this in 2019, and they were married in 1954. If you're doing the math at home, yes, that means my then thirty-two-year-old father married my mother when she was just twenty-two. It's the sort of age gap that would be mildly scandalous today, which is probably why I'm always the lone voice at the water cooler or the cocktail party defending all those "cradle robbers." For me, defending age-gap romance boils down to a defense of my parents' marriage. Whenever someone says something snide, I'm quick to remind them that my own parents have been married for sixty-five freakin' years—so don't tell me that marriages with big age differences can't work!

I firmly believe that my parents' marriage has been successful not in spite of their age gap but because of it. Personality-wise, my parents are very different people. My mother takes crap from no one. She's tough and demanding and fiercely protective of her children and grandchildren.

My father epitomizes mild mannered. He's just a very, very nice man—which is how everyone has always described him. Now, don't get me wrong. My father could be tough when he had to be. He was a successful entrepreneur, and you don't build a business without making difficult choices that piss off a few people along the way. Nevertheless, my father's preference has always been to expect the best of people and treat them accordingly. He exudes patience. He's someone who gains respect by giving it.

In other words, my parents are a textbook example of how opposites attract.

Every marriage has rough patches, of course, and there were definitely times when my mother complained that my father was being too nice. She thought he was being a pushover with friends or family or business associates. She would tell him so rather bluntly. Nevertheless, these arguments were infrequent, and she never pushed disagreements with my father as far as she would with almost anyone else (myself and my brother included). I always found this interesting because my mother has more stamina for arguing than anyone I've ever known, whereas my father generally avoids conflict like the plague. Yet she would let things go with him that she never would with anyone else.

This, I believe, has a lot to do with their age difference. Social mores may have evolved since the 1950s, but the difference in life experience between thirty-two and twenty-two was just as wide in 1954 as it is today. My mother was barely a year out of college on their wedding day. My father, on the other hand, was a World War II vet who fought in Europe. His battalion liberated

Ohrdruf—the first Nazi concentration camp discovered by the Allies. After helping to save the world, he launched a successful career as a chemical engineer. However strong-willed my mother may have been at twenty-two, she just wasn't going to walk all over a thirty-two-year-old with my father's life experience.

Sometimes I wonder if my mother and father would still be married—or would have ever gotten married in the first place—had they been the same age when they first met. I wonder whether my mother would have been able to bite her tongue as readily with a man her own age. I wonder whether she would have trusted a man her own age when he assured her, "Don't worry, I've got this under control." As I see it, the gap in my parents' ages served as a kind of ballast—balancing out the difference between my mother's red-hot personality and my father's much cooler one.

———

I started thinking more deeply about all this after reading a 2017 article on age-gap dating by Dale Markowitz, a data scientist then working for OkCupid. Markowitz's job at OkCupid was to identify trends in dating data that could be helpful for OkCupid users and then to write about these phenomena on OkCupid's blog.

What originally got Markowitz interested in age-gap dating was a news article she had read about the then-newly-elected president of France, Emmanuel Macron. She discovered that Macron's wife, Brigitte, was twenty-four years his senior. The Macrons first met when he was just fifteen—and she was his thirty-nine-year-old drama teacher.

"Not my ideal meet-cute," Markowitz writes, "but whatever—and it made me wonder: Is the old norm of older man with younger woman out?"[18]

The answer turned out to be not really. Though there has been a steady increase in older woman–younger man couples since the 1960s, these pairings remain fairly atypical. In 2017, only 4 percent of married women were married to men at least six years their junior, according to the US Census Bureau. In contrast, 19 percent of married men were married to women at least six years their junior.[19]

Of course, data on all marriages may not be the best way to evaluate whether age preferences are changing among the newly coupled. More than half of married couples stay together at least fifteen years,[20] which means it takes a little while for recent changes in dating mores to show up in the cumulative marriage data. According to census data, age gaps involving older women and younger men are more common among unmarried couples than married ones, which could be a leading indicator of where the marriage data is ultimately headed.

Markowitz decided to do some digging into OkCupid's dating database, and what she discovered surprised her. While lots of men on OkCupid were initiating conversations with much younger women, it generally wasn't working out for them. Younger women ignored older men for the most part. Younger women preferred messages from men their own age.

But when older women initiated conversations with younger men, the dynamic changed dramatically. The older women were actually more likely to get a response from a younger man than from an older man.

"A forty-year-old woman will have better luck messaging a twenty-five-year-old man than a fifty-five-year-old one," Markowitz writes. "And a thirty-year-old man is more likely to respond to a message from a fifty-year-old woman than a message from any other age group.

"To be fair, very few fifty-year-old women (fewer than 1 percent) actually message men this young, but when they do, they kill it . . . When women make the first move, the age-gap dating norm is reversed."[21]

You already know my argument on making the first move. With young women overtaking young men in education and career, it's only natural for these women to take the lead with romance too. Based on the OkCupid report, successful older women should at least consider making the first move with younger men—and not just because young men tend to be fitter and better-looking and, of course, blessed with more sexual stamina.

> "When women make the first move, the age-gap dating norm is reversed."

For starters, there are more of them. Historically, women have married men a few years their senior. While I understand the rationale for this—women favored men who were providers, and older men tended to be more financially secure—the traditional age gap has always had demographic disadvantages for American women. Whenever the population is growing, which has long been the case in the United States, the dating market tends to favor the sex that dates younger.

It boils down to math. As I said earlier, an extreme example involves Baby Boomers. Between the mid-1940s and the mid-1960s, the annual birth rate in the United States increased 25 percent—from twenty live births per capita to twenty-five.[22] Over a twelve-year period, the population of each one-year age cohort in the United States was, on average, 4 percent larger than the one that directly preceded it. From a dating perspective, this wouldn't have mattered if women and men were dating people their own age. But because Baby Boomer women generally dated men three or four years their senior, the dating market became highly imbalanced. In 1967, for example, there were 25 percent more twenty-year-old women born in 1947 than twenty-three-year-old men born in 1944. In her groundbreaking book *Too Many Women?*, Harvard University psychologist Marcia Guttentag attributed the sexual revolution of the 1960s and '70s almost entirely to Baby Boomers' lopsided sex ratio at first marriage.[23] (*Too Many Women?* was finished posthumously by Guttentag's husband, Paul Secord.)

The population may not be growing as quickly today as it was in the 1950s, but reversing the dating age gap can still pay demographic dividends for women, especially college-educated ones who want to marry only college-educated men. In 2011, 34 percent more women than men graduated from US colleges—982,000 women versus 734,000 men, according to the National Center for Education Statistics. In 2015, however, 813,000 men graduated from college, which means the dating math gets a little easier when women dip down agewise.[24] In other words, the sex ratio is 4 women for every 3 men for thirty-one-year-old women dating thirty-one-year-old men, but 5 women for every 4 men for thirty-one-year-old women dating twenty-seven-year-old men. It doesn't solve the problem entirely—the dating market is still lopsided—but it does give women a few more options.

I realize dating by the numbers this way sounds about as romantic as honeymooning in Pyongyang. So let me offer another, perhaps more appealing, explanation for why dating younger men can benefit today's successful women. In much the same way the age gap smoothed over personality differences between my parents, dating younger men can also solve one of the knottiest problems for today's successful women— single men who are intimidated by women's success. Here's how *Cosmopolitan* summarized the problem: "Nearly half the US workforce is female and 40 percent of those women are their family's breadwinner. But as they strive for success, they're hitting a snag. They can't find a guy who's comfortable with all that awesomeness."[25]

When OkCupid's Markowitz interviewed women who'd had success dating younger men, one of the things she discovered was that men were much more comfortable with women's awesomeness when the women were older. "Younger men can't be competitive because we are in completely different life stages," one woman tells Markowitz. Says another: "Men my age can be bossy and authoritative. I have no desire to have a man telling me how I should be conducting my life. A younger man wouldn't dare."[26]

———

I showed Markowitz's article to Lily and Oliver. An executive with a tech startup, Lily is a friend of a friend. Oliver, a photographer and event planner, was her live-in boyfriend at the time I interviewed them. Lily was thirty-five, and Oliver was twenty-seven.

Today they are married with a baby.

Lily and Oliver lived in the same Greenwich Village, New York, neighborhood for years before they ever met. Their apartment buildings were just two blocks apart. They frequented the same neighborhood bar too.

"It's one of those neighborhood spots where everybody knows everybody," Lily says of the bar. "But for whatever reason our paths had never crossed."

"Oh," I reply, "it's like that scene in *When Harry Met Sally* with the old couples . . ."

"'Nine extra floors!'" Lily interrupts. (If you don't get the movie reference, don't worry. Neither did Oliver—which made this the only time during our interview when his age seemed to matter.)

Oliver and Lily met at that neighborhood bar. One evening after work Oliver overheard Lily complaining to the bartender that she had jury duty the next day.

"I had just completed jury duty myself," Oliver recalls, "and it was one of those classic New York City jury duty stories where you go sit in a room all day long, they don't use you for anything, and then you just wasted a whole day.

"I made some joke to her about how she should just show up hammered because they're not going to pick someone who's hammered at eight in the morning."

Lily laughs at the memory. She remembers mentioning to Oliver that she was desperate not to get picked for a jury because she had to make an important presentation at New York University later that week.

"Oh, you're a student," Oliver answered at the time.

"Obviously he thought I was younger than I am!" says Lily.

"I thought you were younger than me!" says Oliver.

Oliver and Lily's retelling of their how-we-met story is filled with fun and warmth and affection. Indeed, everything about our interview told me that Lily and Oliver's relationship was a keeper.

In the end, their age difference turned out to be a nonissue. Oliver says it was never really an issue for him. In fact, when Oliver told his family that he was dating someone older, his brother assumed that meant a woman in her fifties.

"I told him, 'No, she's thirty-five,'" Oliver says. "He was like, 'Oh, whatever.' There was never any judgment."

Lily strikes me as someone who'd be a big hit with parents—smart, kind, responsible, and so on—so I ask Oliver what his parents thought of her.

"Oh my god," he says. "She's the only girl I've dated that my parents actually liked."

Dating younger was more of an issue for Lily, at least at first. Before dating Oliver, Lily had never considered dating someone eight years her junior.

"It never even seemed like a possibility," she says. "When I had an OkCupid account back in the day, I think I had my filter set to [a maximum of] two years younger but ten years older. I don't even know why, other than the fact that's just the norm."

Lily admits she was a little worried about the age difference when they started dating.

"And for all the reasons you'd guess," she says. "All the societal norms. Is he going to think I look old when I'm forty? For some women, there is always that sense of 'Oh, you're thirty, and everything is downhill from there.'"

It's a common fear, yet the latest research on age and beauty calls into question this conventional wisdom. An OkCupid study on how men evaluate women's online dating photos found that men generally perceive single thirty-five-year-old women to be just as attractive as single twenty-five-year-old ones.[27] The only exceptions involved the occasional twentysomething who could pass for a starlet or a model. Of course, those women are out of reach for 99 percent of men anyway. Bottom line: If you're worried a younger man won't find you attractive, don't be.

Lily's other big concern involved lifestyle.

"I was worried about whether I'd be cool enough for you," she says, looking over at Oliver. "I'm sort of lame now. My party years are over. My idea of a fun night is watching a movie and maybe grabbing a glass of wine after. I wasn't sure that would be the same speed as someone who is twenty-seven."

"You can speed up when you want to. I've seen it," Oliver replies.

"I have my moments," she says with a laugh. "But then I have to slow down for a whole week afterward!"

To my ear, Lily's concerns about lifestyle sounded like they had more to do with memories of what her own life was like in her twenties—Lily performed on Broadway when she was younger—as opposed to what Oliver's life is actually like now. As with my parents, the gap in age between Lily and Oliver seemed to make them more compatible, not less so. Had twenty-seven-year-old Lily met twenty-seven-year-old Oliver, I suspect he wouldn't have been cool enough for her, not the other way around. (I'm not dissing Oliver, whom I like a lot—I just suspect Lily ran with a faster crowd during her Broadway days.)

Which brings us back to the issue of men shying away from successful women. Oliver admits that with past relationships, he sometimes had a hard time separating work life from personal life.

"When it comes to the art world, I'm a fiercely competitive person, and sometimes that's been an obstacle with relationships," he says.

Before Lily, Oliver had dated two different women in his field. He says that there were times he felt jealous or resentful when his girlfriends outshined him professionally. He mentions one time in particular when he put his girlfriend in touch with an art buyer he knew—and she ended up landing a gig he'd been angling for. "In my head, I was thinking, 'Fuck you, that should be my gallery show!'" Oliver says.

These sorts of problems never crop up with Lily, even though she is uber-successful. "I've never felt a sense of competition whatsoever," says Oliver.

Because Lily is at a different stage in her career, it's easier for Oliver to feel invested in her success as opposed to threatened by it. He's also comfortable taking career advice from her—and she's comfortable giving it—because they both know she has more experience to draw from.

"I hate to see you ever taken advantage of at work," Lily says. "Sometimes I'm like, 'Speak up about that!' or 'You deserve more money!' or 'Demand the more flexible hours you need!' It's not like you need a cheerleader, but I just feel excited to help you."

"It's okay," Oliver interrupts. "I'll take you as my cheerleader any day."

One thing I did not ask Oliver and Lily about during our first interview was children and fertility. I didn't want to force them into a conversation they probably shouldn't have for the first time with me there. Medical advances may be allowing women to have children at older ages, but egg freezing, IVF, and other fertility treatments are expensive, physically taxing, and not always successful. Indeed, fertility concerns are a reason why some thirty-five-year-old women may be reluctant to date a twenty-seven-year-old man: Her clock is ticking, and maybe he won't be ready for kids in time.

I had hoped Oliver and Lily would bring this up on their own during our interview, but they didn't. Fortunately, Lily texted me about it the next day.

"We thought of one more topic relevant to this conversation and it has to do with fertility," she wrote. "One of the reasons we think this age gap has traditionally been taboo in the past is because we know women become less fertile the older they get."

"I would have asked this question if it were just you," I replied. "But I didn't want to force you guys into a conversation you haven't had yet."

"That makes sense! Appreciate it. [But] we've talked openly about fertility."

Lily told me that before Oliver, she had been on the fence about even having children. But now that Oliver has made it clear that he wants children, Lily now wants them too. Turns out that the difference in their ages pushed Oliver and Lily to have the all-important conversation that too many same-age couples put off.

Given that Lily was already in her midthirties, they decided together that there was no time like the present to start trying to conceive. "He was eager to get going," Lily texted me. "So that's already in motion. :)"

The point here is not that younger men are always better than older men. What I'm saying is that if you close yourself off to the possibility of dating younger men, you eliminate a large pool of dateable, marriageable men who could be exactly what you're looking for.

If you're dating online, my suggestion would be to adjust the age parameters on your filters to include younger men. If you're dating offline, don't be afraid to say yes to younger guys who ask you out. Don't be afraid to ask them out either. You may discover that you have more in common with your twenty-seven-year-old neighbor than with that forty-year-old schmuck you just broke up with.

> **Join the Conversation on the**
> ***Make Your Move* Blog at JonBirger.com**
>
> What's the biggest age gap you'd be comfortable with personally—in either direction? And why?

8

SECOND TIME IS A CHARM

When it comes to "dating who you know," there are no "whos" you'll ever know better than someone you used to date.

Not everybody has an ex-love they still think about, of course. But for those who do, getting back in touch may be a chance worth taking. When exes reunite later in life, these couples fare extremely well the second time around.

Just ask Tania.

A physical therapist in Denver, Tania's love story with her fiancé Derrick began when they were twelve.

"We went to summer camp together," says Tania.

Tania and Derrick lived a few towns apart, which is one reason why they were never precisely boyfriend and girlfriend.

"From ages twelve to seventeen, we were just very, very close," Tania says, "and there were pockets of time when it definitely went far beyond friendship. We just had this very loving friendship in which we experienced a lot of firsts together."

"Not that first," she adds, "though we did talk about it."

Derrick's relationship with Tania was a lone bright spot during a difficult time in his life. He was your textbook troubled teen—in the principal's office way too often and always getting into arguments with his parents at home. It got so bad that Tania's mom even offered to let Derrick live with them just so he could finish up his senior year of high school.

He declined.

Derrick believed his only option was to leave. "He felt he was going to destroy everything—including us—if he didn't get away," Tania says. "He was that boy who had to go off and do whatever it is he thought he had to do in order to find himself.

"He was seventeen when he left. I didn't see him again for twenty years."

The median age for first marriage in the United States is on the rise. It's now thirty for men and twenty-eight for women, up from twenty-three and twenty, respectively, in 1960, according to the Census Bureau.[1] What this means is that lots of first-love relationships like Derrick and Tania's never make it to marriage. Life gets in the way. Maybe parents disapproved and conspired to keep them apart. Maybe she moved away for college or he moved away for work. Maybe they drifted apart naturally, just because nobody expects the person they meet at nineteen or twenty to be their one true love.

The relationships we form in our teens and early twenties have become all too disposable. They've become placeholders. They're learning experiences instead of auditions for potential life partners. Young loves help us discover who we are emotionally and sexually and intellectually, but these boyfriends and girlfriends are usually long gone by the time our journeys of self-discovery are complete.

Perhaps they shouldn't be. Perhaps we should value early romance the same way we value early friendship. Nobody ever questions why you're still best friends with someone you met in middle school or college. Yet throw romance into the mix, and you're told not to get too attached. There are plenty of other fish in the sea.

> Young loves help us discover who we are emotionally and sexually and intellectually, but these boyfriends and girlfriends are usually long gone by the time our journeys of self-discovery are complete. Perhaps they shouldn't be.

"We used to marry when we were seventeen, eighteen," explains Nancy Kalish, professor emeritus of psychology at California State University and the expert on lost-love relationships. "Nowadays," she tells *Quartz*, "there's education, there's other things we do first, and so we're marrying later and we wind up with these lost loves—somebody who, 100 years ago, you would've married at seventeen. Maybe if they'd kept going, they would've been just fine."[2]

Kalish, author of *Lost & Found Lovers: Facts and Fantasies of Rekindled Romances*, became interested in rekindled relationships after reconnecting with an old flame herself. She wound up surveying 1,001 people in fifty states and forty-two countries who had all resumed a relationship with a one-time partner after a minimum of five years apart. Kalish discovered that 72 percent of these recouplings were successful. Another Kalish finding: The older these couples were when they reconnected—and the more years that had passed since they first separated—the more likely these rekindled relationships were to succeed. The classic example is Prince Charles and Camilla—the prince who was not allowed to marry his true love simply because his family did not consider her to be sufficiently virginal or highborn.

"They finally get to 'right the wrong,'" Kalish says of rekindlers. "They feel like this is the person they were meant to be with."[3]

Not every ex is a potential soul mate. But if he's someone you still think about, a lost-love relationship may have more potential than a relationship you start from scratch with a complete stranger you meet on Tinder or Match. Rekindlers build upon real, preexisting connections, often forged at special times in their lives. Again, nobody ever questions why so many of our closest nonromantic friends are people we met in our teens or twenties. So why should anybody be surprised that first or second loves could hold similar importance?

My advice on lost loves does come with an enormous caveat: Personal circumstances matter. I do not want you to break up your own marriage—or worse, break up someone else's—because you've suddenly decided that your college sweetheart is your soul mate. Some mistakes from our past can't be fixed, unfortunately. Perhaps you and he would have lived happily ever after had you stayed together, but if the two of you are not single when you reconnect, there's a good chance that happily-ever-after will elude you. If a rekindled relationship is built upon your own guilt and your spouse's heartbreak, this is not a recipe for lasting happiness. Your new relationship will be forever tainted by betrayal. According to psychologist and infidelity expert Shirley Glass, 75 percent of marriages that begin as extramarital affairs end in divorce.[4]

Kalish found something similar in her own research. Rekindled relationships that begin as extramarital affairs are far less likely to end well than those that begin as two single people reconnecting after years apart. "People who are married agonize over whether to leave their happy marriage to return to the lost love," Kalish says. "If you are happy in your marriage, and don't want to lose it, don't even try. You get torn by two people."[5]

Tania and Derrick never forgot about one another, but they also never forced the other to make a tough choice. Tania moved on with her life after Derrick left home. She graduated from college, launched her physical therapy practice, had long-term relationships, and even got engaged. Sure, Derrick was always there in the back of her mind. But it was, Tania insists, because she genuinely cared about him, not because she believed there would eventually be a fairy-tale ending.

Once or twice a year she would call Derrick's mom to find out how he was doing.

"I just wanted to make sure he was safe," Tania says.

There's an important lesson here for potential rekindlers. People who are just looking for a fling probably aren't going to reach out through a gatekeeper such as a parent. Reconnecting through a parent or a sibling or a mutual friend tends to be an indication of a rekindler's good intentions.

The first time Tania called, Derrick's mom told Tania that Derrick was in New York City working at a fish market. The next time, Derrick's mom didn't know where he was. Another time, he was living in California. A few years later, Derrick's sister called Tania to let her know that Derrick had gotten married.

Derrick and his first wife had two children together. Several years later, Tania heard through the grapevine that the marriage was on the rocks, but she didn't think too much of it because Derrick still lived a thousand miles away. Plus, she and Derrick hadn't actually spoken to one another in fifteen years.

The next time Tania checked in with Derrick's mom, she got a surprise.

"He's here!" she told Tania. "You should come over and say hi."

Even though Derrick's marriage was failing and his wife had stayed back in California, Derrick was still married. And that made him anxious about Tania suddenly showing up on his mom's doorstep after all those years.

"Please don't let her be hot, please don't let her be hot," Derrick remembers thinking.

But Tania was hot (fortunately or unfortunately)—which made this first Derrick-Tania reunion friendly but awkward.

Four more years passed. Tania got engaged in the meantime. But a few months before the wedding, she got into a big row with her fiancé and broke things off. Tania can't say for sure what role Derrick played in her final decision. "Maybe none," she says. But the same night she broke off her engagement, Tania had a vivid dream about Derrick.

"I dreamt I was riding a bike near a beach," Tania recalls. "I went down this hill and ended up getting stuck in this giant puddle, almost up to my waist. I couldn't move. My bike was stuck. I was stuck. My feet were stuck in the sand under the water. Then I heard his voice, and he was saying, 'Tan, let me help you.'

"I turned, and I saw Derrick. I knew it was him because he has a very distinctive voice, but he now had a beard, which he'd never had before. I was just so happy to see him. It's hard to explain, but in that one moment, my entire heart opened up.

"Oh my god, it's finally time!"

"And then I woke up."

Feeling transformed by the dream, Tania proceeded to write Derrick a long email telling him about it. She didn't have huge expectations when she finally hit send. She knew Derrick was divorced, but she had no idea if he was seeing someone.

Derrick's reply: "Oh my god, it's finally time!"

It was a long-distance rekindling at first. Derrick had moved back to Colorado, but Tania had relocated to Charlotte. After weeks of phone calls and emails, she finally flew home to Colorado to see him.

"We ended up talking until three in the morning," Tania said. "The next day, he invited me to go hiking with him and his kids. It could have been awkward, but it was really important for him to have me meet his kids. And I was excited to meet them too.

"It turned out to be great. Weirdly natural. Next thing you know, we're in a long-distance relationship. A few months after that, I moved back to Colorado to be with him."

———

One of the advantages to dating an ex is that you're not holding back emotionally while you try to figure out all the things that may be wrong with him. For Tania, there was never any "Oh, what's it going to be with this one?" She already knew all of Derrick's flaws and foibles. She loved him regardless.

Things that bothered her with other men didn't seem to matter as much with Derrick. For instance, Tania had broken up with a previous boyfriend because he was too much of a workaholic. He always prioritized his job over their relationship. There were too many last-minute cancellations, she says. Too many vacations interrupted by conference calls.

Derrick is also an unrepentant workaholic. Yet Tania tolerates it—maybe even embraces it—because she knows his personal history. As a teenager, Derrick was a searcher. Everyone knew he wasn't cut out for college or a desk job. After dropping out of high school, he crisscrossed the country trying to find his calling. He was a fishmonger at New York's Fulton Fish Market for a while, then a ranch hand in Wyoming, and eventually a carpenter in California. Carpentry stuck, and now Derrick owns and operates a successful woodworking business that makes hand-crafted desks, dining tables, and other home furnishings.

"He's completely and totally dedicated to what he does for a living," Tania says. "To be honest, if it was anyone else and he needed that much freedom, that much time away from me? I'd probably tell him to go fuck himself. But there's something about the foundation we have together that makes it okay with him.

"I understand who he is and where he came from and what he needs—and he loves me for understanding."

> "If it was anyone else and he needed that much freedom, that much time away from me? I'd probably tell him to go fuck himself. But there's something about the foundation we have together that makes it okay with him. I understand who he is and where he came from and what he needs—and he loves me for understanding."

Not everyone has a Derrick. I get that. But Tania and Derrick's love story has so many layers and lessons that it probably deserves its own book. Tania made the first move. It was with someone she already knew. Not only did she know him, but he was her first love. And when they finally got back together, their early history—their "foundation," as Tania puts it—gave their second-chance relationship a massive head start. Some might even call it destiny.

So here's my advice for anyone interested in rekindling an old flame:

1. Always make the first move. In the age of texting and Facebook, getting back in touch with an ex-girlfriend or ex-boyfriend is almost too easy. Nearly every young single woman I know has gotten that Friday afternoon "Hey, what's going on?" text from an ex-boyfriend who's lonely or horny or both.

    Is it possible that he genuinely misses you and thinks you two were meant to be together? Sure, it's possible. But I'd feel a whole lot better about his intentions if he had to jump through a few hoops in order to get back in touch with you. Like asking your mom for your new phone number. Or asking a mutual friend—someone he's accountable to—whether or not you're single. If you make the first move, you won't have to worry about any of this.

2. Don't text him. The advantage of making the first move is that you already know your own intentions (presumably!), whereas you don't know his intentions if he's the one reaching out to you. If you call him or, better yet, if

you speak with him in person, you are much more likely to get a spontaneous, genuine response.

Yes, it would be easier to send a text—and easier on your ego if he responds negatively. But doing this the old-fashioned way is your best defense against his presumption that you're just looking for a hookup. The more you put yourself out there, the more likely it is that he will do the same.

3. Just forget about him if he's married. Or if you are. I'm not trying to be judgy here—I'm just being realistic. Any relationship built on guilt and betrayal is unlikely to succeed—even a rekindled one. Remember that 75 percent of marriages that started as affairs end in divorce. Plus, if your relationship starts out as an affair, you'll never be able to tell your own how-we-met story with the same love and joy that Tania and Derrick tell theirs.

**Join the Conversation on the
Make Your Move Blog at JonBirger.com**

Pop music is filled with songs about lost loves. My personal favorite: "All Summer Long" by Kid Rock. What's yours?

9
UNCHECK THE COLLEGE BOX

ori Stokes is a TV anchor on *Good Day New York*, a morning show on New York City's Fox affiliate. Stokes is successful, she's beautiful, she's charismatic, and it would be totally understandable if she wanted to date only men who are at least as accomplished as she is. Yet Stokes tells the *New York Post*'s Page Six that she has no hard-and-fast rules about whom she'd be willing to date: "I would be open to dating a plumber. All I care is if he's a good person."[1]

Stokes is onto something. If there are too many women in the college-grad dating pool, that means there must be too many men in the non-college-grad pool. In fact, among non-college-grad singles ages twenty-two to twenty-nine, there are now 30 percent more men than women in the United States. We just never hear about this because blue-collar guys do not write novels or screenplays or *Bustle* articles about their dating woes. One of my predictions in *Date-onomics* was that we'll eventually see a lot more of what I dubbed "mixed-collar" marriages—that is, white-collar women married to blue-collar men. (Yes, I realize that "white collar" and "blue collar" are a bit outdated as descriptors. Nevertheless, they're still understood as socioeconomic shorthand—distinguishing today's college-educated workers, who are more likely to hold desk jobs, from today's non-college-educated workers, who are more likely to engage in physical labor.)

I'm an optimist. I refuse to believe that millions of blue-collar men and white-collar women are doomed to loneliness simply because more women than men are attending college. Not everyone appreciates my way of thinking, though. My endorsement of mixed-collar dating turned out to be the most controversial part of *Date-onomics*. David Buss, an evolutionary psychologist at the University of Texas at Austin whom I met at a conference, informed me that most college-grad women will never agree to date blue-collar men and thus a sizable percentage will remain perpetually single. Famed dating coach Evan Marc Katz read an advance copy of *Date-onomics* and warned me that lots of women will hate the idea of dating working-class men.

"Classism," Katz tells me, "is bigger in dating than racism."

One of my Amazon reviewers went so far as to label blue-collar men vultures and criminals. "Let me tell you what's going to happen if you go on a date with Mr. Blue-Collar," this person writes. "On the first date he will lay out a story about why he 'Can't work' and needs you to support him for the rest of his life.

There's a whole range of excuses these Blue-Collar men come up with. 'Bad back.' 'Crohn's disease.' 'Kidney surgery.' 'Record for a petty crime when I was young.' If you are a woman with an education and a home, these vultures will come out of the woodwork. Mr. Blue-Collar wants to move into your house so he can quit his job."

At a Q&A at the Cato Institute, a *Date-onomics* reader who appeared to be in her late twenties complained that she "couldn't imagine having to spend, like, my whole life with [a blue-collar man]—much less having to raise children with him."

I cringed at the remark, yet it drew raucous laughter and applause from this mostly female Washington, DC, audience.

When the *Guardian* published an article about *Date-onomics*, the reporter quoted a London matchmaker, Genevieve Zawada, who says that education is "usually the first thing any woman specifies . . . People think, 'I've dedicated my life to my career and I'm not going to settle for anything less than I am.'"[2] Zawada herself disavows such closed-mindedness—she says, "I think people think that if someone is not educated to the same standards they are, they won't have anything in common, which is absolute nonsense." Problem is, matchmakers are not in the business of telling paying customers what they should or should not want.

I knew *Date-onomics* would never turn mixed-collar romance into the hot new dating trend. But I was still taken aback by the ferocity of the criticism, simply because I personally knew mixed-collar couples with happy marriages. When interviewers or lecture-goers pushed back against my mixed-collar dating advice, I tried not to get overly argumentative or preachy. But over time it became harder and harder for me to be polite.

The final straw came at a book talk I gave in Boston. Several minutes into what was supposed to be a thirty-minute lecture, a woman interrupted with a question. Very quickly my speech morphed into an hour-long Q&A free-for-all.

I listened as educated women, one after another, shared horror stories about men who had used them, lied to them, or cheated on them. One told me about her lawyer boyfriend who'd been telling her for years he'd be ready to get engaged once he turned thirty-five—only to break up with her a few weeks before his birthday. Another woman shared a story about a tech entrepreneur she'd met at a party. They spent a torrid week together, and she thought it was destiny. He neglected to mention that he was about to move to San Francisco.

We talked about the science of sex ratios—how the behavior of educated men has been warped by the college gender gap. The women in the audience seemed relieved to hear that the problem wasn't them. The men in the audience seemed disappointed to find out that their sudden success with women (particularly with women who wouldn't have given them a second look in high school) was not due to their sparkling personalities or their weekend gym routines.

The final question of the evening came from a thirtysomething woman dressed to the nines. She asked for advice on how to identify commitment-minded men who weren't "just looking for a hookup." I explained to her that *Date-onomics* wasn't primarily an advice book, but I did offer her one suggestion from the book that seemed relevant, especially in light of all the horror stories we'd just heard from other women in the room.

"How about dating blue-collar men?" I said. "Maybe the next time you go out with friends, try a fireman's pub instead of a wine bar."

She glared at me like I had just offered her a bowl of wet kibble. "Seriously?" the woman shot back. "You're telling me to settle?"

A long and awkward silence followed.

I wanted to remind her that we'd just heard half a dozen women in the room pour out their hearts about all the terrible, horrible, no-good, very bad, white-collar men they had dated— and yet your takeaway was that not landing one of these guys would be a failure? That marrying a cop or an electrician would be settling?

Instead, I decided to tell her about my wife's friend Cara.

Cara is a high school science teacher in Upstate New York. She graduated from an Ivy League university. She grew up in an upper-middle-class family. Cara always assumed that she would end up marrying a man from that same sort of background. Indeed, those were the only guys Cara ever dated. Problem was, the relationships never seemed to work out, which sometimes led to teary, late-night phone calls to my wife.

At the same time Cara was riding her postcollege romantic roller coaster, she became friendly with a man from work. His name was Pete. A few years older than Cara, Pete was the "director of physical plant" at her high school—which meant Pete was the maintenance guy teachers called whenever a light went out or a toilet clogged or the football field sprinklers would not turn on.

Pete never went to college, but he was smart. He was a former minor league baseball player who passed up a junior college scholarship at eighteen because he was young and foolish and certain he was about to get rich playing pro sports. But baseball didn't work out, which is how he ended up working at the high school and eventually getting to know Cara.

Pete would ask Cara out for dinner every once in a while. Cara would always say no. Pete just didn't seem like the kind of guy she was supposed to be with. But then after one particularly bad breakup with an egomaniacal dermatologist, Cara asked Pete if she could still take him up on the dinner invitation.

Fast-forward to the present day, and Cara and Pete have been married for twenty-five years. My wife and I used to socialize with Cara and Pete when we lived in the same area, and I can tell you that Pete set a high bar for other young husbands. He was affectionate and supportive, fit and good-looking. He knew how to fix a leaky sink as well as change the oil in Cara's car. (The rest of us were really good at using the Yellow Pages.) He also didn't seem as anxious about the future as the rest of us—

"Trust me, I didn't settle. I think I hit the jackpot."

perhaps because he didn't have thousands of dollars in college or law-school debt weighing on his mind. Best of all, Pete turned out to be a phenomenal dad.

I told Cara and Pete's story to the woman in Boston because I wanted to drive home the point to her that a college degree does not make someone a better wife or husband. I told her that my head would explode if anybody ever suggested to Cara and Pete's son that his mom had "settled" or "compromised" or "married down" when she married Pete. I told her that Cara herself hears cruel remarks like this all the time. Cara's standard response? "Trust me, I didn't settle. I think I hit the jackpot."

―――

The world is changing, even if some people can't see it. According to US Census data, the percentage of heterosexual couples in which the woman outearns the man has risen from 16 percent in 1981 to 29 percent in 2018.[3] And the actual number is almost definitely higher than 29 percent. A 2018 Census Bureau study found that couples tend to overreport men's income and underreport women's whenever women are primary breadwinners.[4]

You see the change in the latest data on marriage and education too. A Pew Research Center study on couples with differing levels of education found that 60 percent of women ages thirty to thirty-four are now better educated than their husbands, compared to 42 percent in 1970.[5] In other words, it's now more likely that a female lawyer will marry a hunky construction worker than that a male lawyer will marry a secretary.

You see it in popular culture. *Sex and the City* featured two mixed-collar couples: lawyer Miranda and bartender Steve, and journalist Carrie and furniture maker Aidan. The Netflix rom-com *Always Be My Maybe* is built around the relationship between white-collar Sasha and blue-collar Marcus. And just about every Tyler Perry movie seems to feature a professional woman coupled with a blue-collar guy with a heart of gold.

You see it in dating blogs and in lifestyle media. Over at The Good Men Project, a media company and social platform based around cultural conversations about manhood, Colorado attorney and relationship writer Blixa Scott blogs about her frustrations with friends and family—"including [her] own mother"—who cannot understand why she loves her blue-collar boyfriend so much. "I've been offered a variety of theories to explain my behavior," she writes. "One is that I'm a sex fiend and my man is more boy-toy than boyfriend. Another is that deep down I have low self-esteem and don't think I deserve better . . .

"All of these people believe that my relationship is a passing fancy and that eventually, when I'm done playing games, I'll take the mature route and settle down with a man deemed socioeconomically appropriate. What they can't seem to wrap their heads around is the fact that my guy's working-class job is not some detriment or novelty that I'm temporarily willing to indulge. To the contrary, it's a distinct benefit."[6]

Why is it a benefit? Scott offered three explanations:

1. He's fun. "The nature of my boyfriend's work gives him the freedom to let loose and be himself in a way that that many professionals just can't afford to do, and that makes him far better company."

2. He's happy. "My job is good for generating income, but it's not particularly good at generating happiness. Lawyers are a notoriously miserable bunch. The long hours, solitary work, and necessity of tracking your time in

six-minute increments produce enormous stress." Scott is mentally taxed at the end of the day, whereas her boyfriend is unburdened. "Because he's paid by the hour, there's no taking work home. When he's off the clock, he's free. He isn't expected to constantly check his email or field conference calls. He doesn't have to go in on the weekend to impress his boss (and if he did, he would get overtime, not just brownie points). In general, he doesn't worry about work unless he's working. His time is his own."

3. He's sexy. "This one is simple: a physical job leads to a great physique. I used to wonder how he could maintain such a great body without ever doing exercise, until he reminded me that he does slow but steady exercise all day long. He has no reason to go to the gym when he spends eight hours every day squatting, climbing, and lifting."

A lifestyle piece in the *New York Post* makes many of the same points. It spotlights white-collar women whose "solution to NYC's man drought"—a concept the *Post* borrows from *Date-onomics*—is to "date down."[7] Personally, I try to stay away from describing mixed-collar dating as "dating down." The phrase strikes me as pejorative and unkind. But verbiage aside, the *Post* story does capture mixed-collar dating's appeal.

For starters, it's easier to decompress after work with a man who doesn't bring his work home with him (literally or figuratively). Taryn, a twenty-eight-year-old research scientist, met her blue-collar fiancé, Eric, in the Long Island barber shop he runs. "I'm a pretty strict, Type A person at work, but I feel I can just turn that off at home," she tells the *Post*. "With my fiancé, I feel I can relax."

"I always tended to go for the 'man's man,' which I just wasn't finding at college," she continues. "I also think the fact we have different professional backgrounds is a huge advantage. If I had settled down with a doctor or fellow scientist, I'm sure there would be some competition."

Andrea, a thirty-one-year-old lawyer married to an electrician, tells the *Post* that other women wrongly assume that blue-collar men won't pull their weight financially. "I think there's a common misconception that 'lack of a degree' means 'lack of income,' which isn't the case," she says. "I have student-loan debt, which my husband doesn't have. He's doing really well, financewise."

"My husband is successful, driven, and a devoted dad," Andrea notes. "What more could I want?"

———

I do understand why some women may balk at dating working-class men. Even my wife's friend Cara did initially. And remember, I'm the guy who just told you to date who you know. In an America increasingly segregated by income and education, white-collar women just don't know a lot of blue-collar men. The sharp rise in economic inequality since the 1960s has resulted in less mingling between college grads and noncollege grads, according to a 2010 Brown University study.[8] Mixed-income neighborhoods are disappearing, while the percentage of

Americans living in economically homogeneous neighborhoods has doubled.

Bottom line: It's hard for sparks to fly if you never even rub elbows.

Despite the obstacles, I'm doubling down on my mixed-collar dating advice. I urge you to open your hearts and minds to the possibility of dating men who shower after work rather than before. There are a lot of good ones out there. They're hardworking. They're loyal. They're take-charge. As Andrea said, they probably make more money than you think they do. Plus, depending on their hours, their workday is likely to be over before yours, which means they've got more time for you—and for the kids someday. Speaking as a baseball dad, I can tell you that some of the best Little League coaches I know are cops and contractors.

> I urge you to open your hearts and minds to the possibility of dating men who shower after work rather than before. There are a lot of good ones out there. They're hardworking. They're loyal. They're take-charge. They probably make more money than you think they do.

Some of you are probably wondering why my push for mixed-collar dating seems more directed at women than men. It's a fair question. It's not because I think college-grad men are any more open-minded than college-grad women. They are not.

Contrary to popular belief, very few college-grad men end up marrying secretaries or cocktail waitresses. College-educated men are actually less likely than college-grad women to marry someone without a college degree. Among recent newlyweds, 32 percent of college-educated women married someone with less education than them versus only 20 percent of college-educated men, according to a 2018 study published by the *Annual Review of Sociology*.[9]

The only reason my mixed-collar dating advice is more directed at women is because, on account of the college gender gap, mixed-collar dating carries strategic advantages for college-grad women that don't really apply to college-grad men. When educated men discriminate against non-college-grad women, it does not diminish their dating prospects. The excess supply of college-grad women is just so vast—four women for every three men—that there's no penalty for men who refuse to date women who didn't go to college.

The opposite is true for college-grad women. When educated women refuse to date blue-collar men, they wind up limiting themselves to a dating pool with too few men. Making matters worse, the longer that educated men remain single, the more likely they are to exploit the imbalance. According to University of Washington sociologist Pepper Schwartz, educated men are less likely to be monogamous at age forty than their blue-collar peers,[10] which is one reason I believe giving all those doctors and lawyers and bankers a little more competition is so important.

So how do you go about finding hunky cops and construction workers? As you know, I'm not a huge fan of online dating. But if you are going to date online (and I know many of you will, regardless of what you've read here), I do have a suggestion: Uncheck the college box. That's what Jennifer Weber did. Jennifer tweeted me after reading a *New York Post* article about *Date-onomics*. "I found my husband after I unchecked education on dating sites," she writes. "Many of my friends with grad degrees did too . . ."[11]

Keep in mind that even after you expand your online dating filters to include non-college men, the same drawbacks to online dating will still apply. You'll still have to wade through the fraudsters and weirdos and super-awkward first dates. But the good news is that you will have expanded your pool of dateable men to include more men who are monogamy-minded.

Want an offline way to find blue-collar men? Go where they are. (This particular bit of dating advice probably applies to all men, not just blue-collar types.) As I said before, I've been amazed at the number of women I've met on the lecture circuit who complain that they took their mom's or their sister's or their married friend's advice and joined a book club or a cooking class in order to meet men. They're frustrated it didn't work out. My response: Of course you didn't meet any men—because there are very few straight, single men in book clubs or cooking classes!

Or in any type of group class, it seems. Here's what the *New York Times* has to say on this topic: "No one denies that love occasionally blooms during Thai kickboxing or jazz appreciation . . . Still, grumbles about the lack of single men in group classes are not unfounded. Professionals who oversee classes in

New York suggested that men tend to avoid group instruction, particularly beginner classes, because they think they should already know all about, say, sports or wine. Those who do seek instruction, they said, generally prefer private lessons."[12]

If you're looking for activities with single men, my advice would be to skip the book clubs and the jazz appreciation classes and invest in a softball mitt instead. I've met a bunch of women who told me they met their husbands or boyfriends playing in coed softball leagues or other sports leagues (flag football, soccer, and so on). The opportunities for first encounters of the close kind are endless with team sports.

Guy gets injured sliding into home plate. Girl gets the first aid kit and cleans up the cut. Sparks fly.

Girl scores the winning goal. Celebratory hugs follow. Cue the music.

You get the picture.

What if playing team sports isn't your thing? Well, how about watching them? Guys do love their sports (as do lots of women), and it's easy to see how the shared camaraderie of rooting on your team might beget romance. Ohio experienced a huge marriage boom one year after the Cleveland Cavaliers gave the state its first-ever professional sports championship. The number of Ohio women walking down the aisle increased 9 percent between 2016 and 2017, according to the Census Bureau.[13] Coincidence? I think not!

That said, I wouldn't walk into just any sports bar and start scanning the room for Mr. Rights. That's a daunting task, especially for someone shy or introverted. I've got a better idea, one that is more targeted. It involves my absolute favorite website for dating, even though this website isn't actually a dating site.

It's Meetup.com.

For anyone unfamiliar with Meetup, the site is basically a city-by-city directory of online groups that host in-person events for people with shared interests—rock climbers, dog lovers, sports fans, and the like. The sports-fan Meetups almost always take place at sports bars. Not everyone who attends a Meetup will be single, of course, but that may be a good thing. It's often easier for singles to get to know each other in settings where there's less pressure to connect. Best of all, Meetups come standard with super-easy icebreakers. ("Hi, I'm Trish. Are you here for the Lakers fan Meetup? Me too! What's your name?")

Plan ahead, and join a Meetup (or two or three) for your favorite sports team or teams. It's an easy way to make new friends—and perhaps even a special friend too.

———

Sometimes you don't have to plan ahead in order to date outside the box. Sometimes opportunities just present themselves. The key is being prepared to say yes when the right one comes along.

That's what happened to Seleana Bines. Seleana is a *Date-onomics* reader whom I met in 2017, after she penned a relationship column for the *Washington Post*. Her headline: "How I Realized It Was Okay to Date a Man Less Educated Than I Am."[14]

A thirtysomething divorcée living in Washington, DC, Seleana was struggling with postdivorce dating. She'd had two kinda-sorta relationships—one with a doctor, another with a senior official at the Pentagon—but neither gentleman seemed terribly eager to move things along from casual dating to a serious relationship. Seleana hoped to get married again, but the men she was dating seemed perfectly happy with the status quo.

"The college-educated men I've dated did not have marriage on the forefront of their life plan," Seleana writes. "I knew that I had to make a few adjustments to my approach in dating."

The adjustments were not easy. Seleana always assumed she'd end up with another high achiever (she's an executive at a top public relations agency). The doctor and the Pentagon official looked good on paper, which is why she continued to go out with them despite the fact that they seemed to take her for granted. She continued to pursue relationships with them, she tells me, because she "thought there was compatibility."

Seleana is African American, and she believes it's especially hard for African American women who are educated and successful to accept the idea of not marrying someone who is at least as accomplished as they are. "There's so much history," she explains, "so much that has burdened us in the black community. We feel like we're always playing catch-up. Because of that legacy, the community drills in us the importance of going to college, of getting your education.

"And when it comes to marriage, the message may not always be to marry up but there's certainly pressure not to fall back either."

Thing is, Seleana wasn't having much luck with the men she thought she was supposed to be with. Her friends all had similar complaints.

"Some of my friends hit their fortieth birthday and literally feel like they can't wake up out of bed—they feel like they've missed out," Seleana tells me. "We talk openly about the problem. 'We're successful. We're attractive. Why aren't we able to settle down?'"

Their first thought was to blame geography.

"We thought the problem might be the DC area," she says. "But then one of my friends moved to Atlanta and experienced exactly the same thing there."

Seleana knew there was a shortage of college-educated men—the college gender gap is especially wide in the African American community—but she and her friends weren't prepared to put all the blame on men for their dating woes.

"My friends and I just sat down and decided that maybe we're looking at this a bit wrong," she says. "Let's look at who's going to make a great husband and a great father. We stopped going for the men everyone else was going for.

"And guess what? We're now all engaged or married. And just to be clear, it's not about settling. It's about being intentional. About finding the partner who's right for you."

That was Seleana's mindset one night in February 2017 when she pulled into the parking garage at DC's Ronald Reagan Federal Building for an evening event. Suddenly she found herself locking eyes with the very handsome security guard manning the entrance.

"Good morning," he said to her.

"It's evening," she replied with a smile.

There was something about the security guard's slipup—specifically the nervousness behind it—that she found appealing. It emboldened her to take a chance.

She asked his name and then asked him if he was single.

Answers: Greg. And yes.

She then asked for his phone number.

"The bold act was out of character for me, and I second-guessed it immediately," Seleana writes. "He must've sensed my internal struggle and asked me to text him, so that he could have my phone number. I did. It was simply, 'This is Seleana.'"

He texted back minutes later. "Your smile made my day," he wrote.

Seleana and Greg started dating. He turned out to be spiritual, hardworking, family oriented—all the things Seleana prioritized on her "husband list." Equally important, Greg was marriage-minded. Three weeks after they started dating, Greg asked Seleana to date him exclusively. Two months after, Greg and Seleana met each other's families. Eight months after, Greg got down on one knee and proposed.

Seleana said yes. Greg and Seleana were married in 2018.

Seleana can't say for sure that being on the wrong side of the college gender gap had made Greg more marriage-minded than all the white-collar men she had dated. It could just be who Greg is. Either way, she loved the fact that Greg was intent on building a life together with her, which had not been the case with the white-collar men she'd dated.

"He's been my Superman," Seleana says of Greg. "At one point early in our relationship, my daughter became sick, and he stepped up and became that support very quickly."

Greg's presence also made it easier for Seleana to advance professionally.

"After my divorce, there were opportunities when I wouldn't even raise my hand, just because who's going to help me watch my daughter if I need to travel?" Seleana says. "Greg's situation is more steady, with more regular hours. So if I do need to travel or stay late, he is there to support me. And he's happy to support me, which I appreciate."

I ask Seleana if, after she got engaged, she'd ever heard back from the doctor or the Pentagon official. I wanted to test out my theory that college-educated men might change their ways if they knew they had competition.

"Yeah, absolutely," she tells me. "[The Pentagon official] was very respectful about it. He realized he may have missed an opportunity."

**Join the Conversation on the
Make Your Move Blog at JonBirger.com**

My favorite non-dating dating site is Meetup.com. What's yours?

10

THE RELUCTANT GROOM

Okay, so you've found your guy, you've been together a few years, and things are going great. There's just one problem: You're ready to get married, but he's in no rush. What you've got is a reluctant groom problem.

It's a familiar dilemma for lots of college-educated, marriage-minded women. You're afraid to rock the boat. You don't want to scare off the man you love by nagging him about marriage. I get it. I've had friends in this predicament. (Hasn't everyone?) Problem is, too many women end up wasting big chunks of their twenties and thirties on men who feel no guilt or shame about running out their partners' biological clocks.

"Time thieves—that's what I call these guys," Maria Avgitidis, a top New York City matchmaker, once told me.

The reluctant groom problem would be a heck of a lot easier to solve if so many women weren't hung up on the Hollywood ending. Women want their guys to come around on their own. They want men to have a "You're the one!" epiphany. They want the perfect diamond ring presented at the perfect moment with the perfect words in the perfect location.

Question is, how long is too long to wait for the Hollywood ending?

One woman I know waited five years for a proposal that would never come. She wound up freezing her eggs and having a baby on her own years later.

Nobody is obligated to get married, of course. If you're hoping I'm going to provide you with magic words that will forever change the minds of men (or women) who have been honest and forthright about not wanting to get married, you might as well skip this chapter. Marriage and monogamy are not for everyone. Nobody should be tricked or coerced into walking down the aisle.

That said, most of the over-thirty reluctant grooms I've known were never philosophically opposed to marriage. They just kept insisting that they weren't yet "ready" to get married. From what I could see, their readiness was directly tied to the man deficit. Once these men turned thirty, an ever-increasing number of single, attractive, college-educated women were suddenly vying for their attention. Instead of making them more inclined to settle down, turning thirty had just opened their eyes to new possibilities. "I was much more cavalier about breaking up with women," one guy told me. For men like this, "not ready" had become a euphemism for "Why should I make a lifetime commitment to one woman when I can keep her as an option while continuing to survey the market?"

If this is your predicament, you need to stop waiting and start acting. Your man may be a good guy who just needs a little push. Or he could be a jerk who needs to be cut loose. Either way, you need to find out. Your action plan for solving the reluctant groom problem starts here.

Control the Clock on Your Relationship

Yes, it would be better if the love of your life came around on his own. But you cannot waste your twenties and thirties waiting for the fairy-tale ending. Some men are oblivious to their partner's biological-clock concerns (especially now that medical advances allow women to extend their fertility). Others have been so warped by the man deficit that they think they're special and thus entitled to special consideration. They're not bad guys—they just need to be brought back to reality.

So don't be scared. Be proactive. If your relationship is stuck in neutral, stop being satisfied with the status quo. If you want to get married, you need to make that clear to him.

Don't be scared. Be proactive. If your relationship is stuck in neutral, stop being satisfied with the status quo. If you want to get married, you need to make that clear to him.

The question is how to do so. In *Date-onomics*, I advised women in this predicament to give their guys a marriage ultimatum. It wasn't long before I wished for a literary do-over.

My advice in *Date-onomics* seemed straightforward enough. Give him a firm deadline for proposing. A month or two or three. If the deadline passed without a proposal, then it was time to part ways. No matter the outcome, it's still a win. If the ultimatum works, you're married to the man you love. If not, at least you won't waste another year on a man who cannot commit long term.

A few *Date-onomics* readers have told me they took my advice and were pleased with the results. "You're my angel!" one woman wrote me. "I'm engaged and getting married in April. :)"

Over time, however, I came to see the marriage ultimatum as the wrong solution to the right problem. Some readers complained that *Date-onomics* was the least romantic book they'd ever read about dating, and my marriage ultimatum advice seemed to prove their point. Where's the romance in telling a guy to put a ring on it or else? Proposal stories are supposed to be joyful. As famed LA matchmaker Julie Ferman reminds me, "She's going to be telling people for the rest of her life about this beautiful way that her husband proposed to her and how much he loved her."

Giving a guy a marriage ultimatum turns what is supposed to be a joyful memory into a joyless negotiation. In hindsight, I allowed sexist gender roles and gender norms to shape my advice. I couldn't imagine anything other than a traditional marriage proposal. To my way of thinking, the only way to get a man to the altar was to get him to propose. I now see a much better way, one that pushes men to decide but does not spoil the engagement magic. My new advice: Don't demand that he propose to you.

Ask him to marry you.

Yes, Propose to Him

That's what Katie Burton did, and Katie has been a one-woman advocacy group for women proposing to men ever since.

A London journalist in her late twenties when I interviewed her, Katie had been thinking about proposing to her boyfriend, Chris, for months before she finally popped the question. Katie and Chris were college sweethearts, and after being together for eight years, Katie was getting a little tired of waiting for Chris to get down on bended knee. Plus, everyone was sure that Katie and Chris were going to get married eventually, and in Katie's mind, that was a problem in and of itself.

"Let's just say I wouldn't have been bowled over if he had asked me," Katie says with an infectious laugh. (Over the phone, Katie sounds like one of those quirky characters from a Hugh Grant rom-com.)

Katie wanted her engagement to be special. To be memorable. She wanted it to be a story she and Chris could tell the kids and grandkids someday. But because Katie and Chris were already deemed a matched set by friends and family, Katie worried that Chris's proposal to her would prove anticlimactic. Everyone's not-so-funny take would be something along the lines of "What took him so long?"

Hers was not an idle concern. According to *Cosmopolitan*, nearly a third of women report saying no to a man's proposal simply because they did not like the way he proposed.[1] Another survey identified "unromantic proposal setting" as the number-one reason why women say no to marriage proposals.[2] It may sound petty to reject a guy simply because he proposed in the Trader Joe's parking lot instead of on the beach in Antigua. But marriage proposals are about more than just the asking and answering of a question. A 2007 University of Iowa study found that people perceive couples with good proposal stories to have stronger relationships.[3] Proposals are defining chapters in a couple's "story of us." When a couple's proposal story is compelling—when it epitomizes everything special about their relationship—they and everyone around them become more invested in the relationship's success.

It's why so many people look for signs from above that the mate choice they're making is the right one. People want existential proof before walking down the aisle. A falling feather perhaps. A favorite love song coming on the radio at just the right moment. And what if a marriage proposal falls flat? Maybe that's a sign from above that the relationship was not meant to be.

Katie never planned out the how and when of proposing to Chris. She just waited for the right moment and then found it during a ski vacation in the Alps with Chris and a group of friends. Standing at the top of the mountain (and admittedly feeling emboldened by a midday gin and tonic), Katie wondered aloud to her best friend if she should propose to Chris after their next run.

"I think this might be good!" her friend said.

"Oh gosh," Katie replied, "I guess we'll find out!"

Katie found Chris back at the ski lodge. She captures what happened next in a column penned for *HuffPost UK*. Her headline: "I Will Never Regret Proposing to My Boyfriend—More Women Should Pop the Question."[4]

"I was standing on a giant beanbag, my heart hammering so hard I suspected an imminent seizure," Katie writes. "Everyone was staring at me. This is an interesting turn of events, I thought.

"I got down on one knee (note to the wary, this is a bad idea on a giant beanbag), and I proposed marriage to my boyfriend. My mate couldn't believe it . . . It was unbelievable. My boyfriend looked flabbergasted, which is a very funny look on a man dressed in a vintage onesie."

However flabbergasted Chris may have been, he still answered with a very enthusiastic "yes"—which prompted everyone around them to burst into cheers. Katie writes: "A man who can't find the joy in being proposed to might end up a real buzz-kill!"

A story that could have ended with "What took him so long?" was transformed into "Katie loved Chris so much that she asked him to marry her!"

For Katie, the experience was incredibly empowering. "Seriously, you will dine on the glory forever," Katie says. "Don't ask me why, it's just the way it is."

The ultimate goal of asking a man to marry you is no different from giving him a marriage ultimatum. The goal is to get married. But just imagine if Katie had given Chris an ultimatum instead of proposing to him. There would have been no cheers at the ski lodge. No joyful toasts from friends and strangers. No great story to tell the kids. Just a long, hard conversation that probably would have put a serious damper on their ski holiday.

Where's the magic in that?

The big difference between a marriage proposal and a marriage ultimatum is that one involves being asked and the other being told. Everyone likes to be asked, whereas nobody likes to be told. It's how the human brain is wired. Other animal species may not mind being bossed around—when is the last time you heard of a worker bee demanding to be a drone?—yet most humans hate taking orders. Early man evolved in hunter-gatherer societies that were much more egalitarian than the ones we live in today, according to Peter Gray, a research psychologist at Boston College. It's why modern humans chafe against hierarchy and inequality. "Nobody had the right to tell others what to do," Gray writes of early hunter-gatherer culture. "Even parents didn't have the right to order their children around."[5]

> The big difference between a marriage proposal and a marriage ultimatum is that one involves being asked and the other being told. Everyone likes to be asked, whereas nobody likes to be told. It's how the human brain is wired.

Nowadays, there's always going to be someone in charge—a boss, a mayor, a coach, a teacher, and so on. Yet even if most of us accept hierarchy as necessary, that doesn't mean we have to like being told what to do. This push and pull between what individuals want and what civilization requires is one of the things that makes modern leadership so complicated. It's why the adage about catching more flies with honey than vinegar has always been Management 101 gold.

My point here is this: You're more likely to get the response you want by asking your man to marry you than by telling him it's time for him to propose. And if you're worried he's going to say no just because you did the asking, please don't be. Much the same way the human brain is hardwired to recoil at being given orders, it's also predisposed to respond positively when the person doing the asking does so nicely. Consider it an offshoot of "the beautiful mess effect" we talked about in Chapter 5.

Stanley Milgram, a psychology professor at City University of New York, put this theory to the test in a famed 1974 study. Milgram assigned a team of students to ask strangers on the New York City subway a seemingly nutty question: "Can I have your seat?"

There was no reason for any of the subway riders to say yes. The students were not elderly or pregnant or disabled or sick (though the assignment itself made some students queasy: "I thought I was going to throw up," one of Milgram's researchers reports). They simply asked people on the subway if they could have their seats and then waited politely for a reply.

The result? Sixty-eight percent of New York City subway riders gave up their seats without hesitation. But when the question askers were rude or demanding, the percentage saying yes dropped to 38 percent.[6] Reporters from both the *New York Times* and London's *Independent* replicated Milgram's experiment in

2004—in honor of the study's thirty-year anniversary—and both newspapers found that subway riders today are even more likely to give up their seats than they were in 1974.[7]

People want to say yes. That's why, if your guy says no, it won't be simply because you were the one who popped the question. There hasn't been a ton of research on women proposing marriage, but surveys that have been done show that men are no less inclined to say yes to proposals than are women. A 2015 *Glamour* poll found that 70 percent of men would be "psyched" if their girlfriends proposed to them.[8] A 2016 survey conducted in the United Kingdom found that 73 percent of men would like to be proposed to.[9]

What Happens If He Does Say No?

The important thing to remember is it won't be because you were the one who proposed. It will be because he doesn't want to marry you. Finding that out will hurt. It will hurt a lot. It will keep you up at night. And I'm so sorry if this is your experience. But trust me, you'll be better off in the end. You'll be better off knowing that he did not love you the same way you loved him. And you won't be wasting another year on a guy who won't commit to you.

Now, is it possible his rejection might include some hurtful remarks about you proposing? Absolutely, it's possible. But please, please do not believe for a second that the relationship would have worked out had you not asked him to marry you.

Trust me, any guy who rejects you after you tell him you want to spend the rest of your life with him is not the guy for you. The relationship was never going to work out. There was never going to be a happily-ever-after.

Breakups are not exit interviews. The goal for the breaker-upper is not to provide a full accounting of everything he thinks went wrong with the relationship. The goal is merely to end the relationship with as little drama and recrimination as possible. A truly honest explanation might be, "Honestly, I knew a year ago that I didn't love you enough to marry you, but I was too lazy to find someone else." Thing is, most cads aren't actually caddish enough to say such a thing (especially now that bad breakup tales get splashed all over social media). It's so much easier to just flip the blame around.

Make New Traditions

I know what some of you are thinking: Men propose to women, not the other way around. That's the way it's always been, and that's the way it always will be.

But have you ever asked yourself what's behind this one-sided tradition?

For most of human history, women had no control whatso-ever over whom they married or when. England's King Edward II, for example, married Isabella of France when she was just twelve. Marriage, according to social historian Stephanie Coontz, author of *Marriage, a History*, originated as a kind of barter.[10] It was used to settle debts or to acquire property, protection, or alliances. There was never any doubt that men were the ones who initiated marriage because women were never party to the transaction. Women were the ones being transacted.

And from that ugly history emerged the modern tradition of men proposing marriage to women.

By the early twentieth century, most women in the West could choose whether or not to say yes to a marriage proposal, yet it was still considered taboo for them to actively seek out their preferred mate. The assumption was that women were too emotional—too irrational—to choose a spouse on their own. "Women's supposed desperation to marry made Americans believe that men were more rational," says Katherine Parkin, a cultural historian at Monmouth University, in a news article on the history of marriage.[11]

Today we recognize such thinking as outdated crap, so why do we still abide by its legacy? Why, at a time when women are leading countries and running Fortune 500 companies, do we blindly accept the notion that women cannot propose marriage? If General Motors CEO Mary Barra can negotiate a labor contract with the UAW and if German chancellor Angela Merkel can hash out a truce between Ukraine and Russia, shouldn't they also be able to ask a man to marry them?

Katie Burton certainly thinks so. She sees women proposing marriage as a long overdue revision of sexist gender roles. "It's your fast-pass to badass feminism," she writes.[12]

One of the United States' most prominent politicians evidently feels the same way.

"I proposed to Bruce in a classroom," Elizabeth Warren, US senator from Massachusetts and former presidential candidate, wrote on Facebook in 2016.[13]

Warren's Facebook post was an open anniversary message to her law-professor husband, Bruce Mann.

"It was the first time I'd seen him teach," writes Warren, herself a former law professor. "I was already in love with him, but watching him teach let me see one more thing about him—and that was it. When class was over and the students had cleared out, he came up to me and asked somewhat hesitantly, 'Uh, what did you think?'"

Warren's reply: "What can I say? Will you marry me?"

"He stared back at me," Warren continues. "It was not the first (or last) time that I gobsmacked him . . . But he blinked a couple of times, then jumped in with both feet. 'OK.'

"To make sure the deal was sealed, I smiled and said, 'Good. Let's do it.'

"It made no sense at all. Bruce was teaching in Connecticut, and I was teaching in Houston. And besides, there was the small matter of the fact that I had a complicated life: two children, both of my parents and my Aunt Bee popping in and out all day, a red station wagon and a mean little dog that bit people. Bruce had lived with none of the above—children, seniors, station wagons, or dogs—but he never hesitated.

"We got married thirty-six years ago today. It made no sense at all, but maybe that's how love works. All I know is that I'm sure glad I asked—and sure glad he said yes.

"Happy anniversary, Sweetie! I love you."

You Don't Have to Act Like a Man to Propose to One

One of the many remarkable things about Elizabeth Warren's marriage proposal to Bruce Mann was its simplicity. There was no string quartet playing in the background. No private beach. No vanilla-scented candles leading to a heart-shaped bed of roses. She didn't even have a ring. Were a man to propose marriage this casually, his own mother might give him a smack.

Yet despite the total lack of fanfare, Mann never hesitated about saying yes. He never complained that she was proposing in a dingy classroom or that she had failed to get down on one knee. That's because men have zero expectations when it comes to proposals. Men don't expect anyone to propose to them, which means you're not competing against his fantasy of what a proposal is supposed to be. No man is going to pass judgment if your proposal lacks sufficient pizzazz. Borrowing a word from Warren, he'll be "gobsmacked" no matter how you ask.

I'd argue that there's so much pressure nowadays on men to nail the proposal—and so much judgment if they get it wrong—many couples would actually be happier if the woman did the asking. Lorraine Sayers and William Wilkinson certainly were.

A mom in Sussex, England, Sayers proposed to her live-in beau on live radio. Both she and Wilkinson were thrilled that she did.

Great Britain and Ireland have a silly but longstanding tradition of women being "allowed" to propose to men once every four years, on Leap Day. (You may recall the 2010 Amy Adams movie *Leap Year*.) Sayers decided to take the Leap Day plunge on a morning radio show. She explains that she was tired of waiting for Wilkinson to pop the question. "After nine years together and no ring I thought it was time I took matters into my own hands!" says Sayers.[14]

Not only did Wilkinson say yes, but he was quite thankful Sayers had asked. Says Wilkinson, "I really love her and I'm so glad she proposed. She beat me to it."[15]

Public proposals tend to be giant no-no's when women are on the receiving end. Some recent headlines on the subject include "Public Marriage Proposals Must Die,"[16] "Let's Just Be Honest, Public Proposals Are NOT Romantic,"[17] "Proposing in Public Is the Worst and You Should Never Do It,"[18] and "Public Proposals: True Romance or Unwarranted Coercion?"[19] Yet Wilkinson did not balk or complain when Sayers put him on the spot on live radio. He was just tickled to be asked.

That's because a woman proposing to a man doesn't have to conform to any rules. And because there are no rules, a woman's proposal can be simultaneously feminist and feminine. Julie Ferman, the veteran matchmaker, shared her own story to explain how.

Ferman proposed to her own husband, Gil.

Well, she kind of proposed.

"Gil prefers to call it 'the conversation that got out of control,'" Ferman says with a laugh.

The one thing she and Gil agree on is that "the conversation that got out of control" foretold the very happy marriage to come.

The story began in the late 1980s, when Ferman was twenty-seven and living in St. Louis, Missouri. Back then, Ferman was like a lot of single women today. She was working crazy hours in a high-powered job (she was national sales director for the Ritz-Carlton hotel chain). Marriage and family had always been part of her life plan, but they'd been on the back burner simply because she didn't have a lot of time for dating.

Then a medical scare shifted her priorities.

"I had surgery to remove one and a half of my ovaries," Ferman says, "and suddenly it occurred to me that I better get busy. So I treated it like a job. I put together a personal profile with photos. I went to Staples and had a zillion copies made, and I sent five of them to everyone in my contacts list, with a cover letter that read, 'Who do you know who wants to meet this girl?'"

She wound up going out on fifty blind dates over two years, but none of the men were quite right. She'd been targeting alpha men—"men who were bigger and stronger and made a lot of money"—but back then, those men were looking for a Robin to their Batman. They wanted someone to stay home with kids.

"They didn't want to come home to boss lady," says Ferman.

Two years of nonstop dating failed to yield the desired result, and Ferman was getting worried. One night Ferman found herself alone at an Ethiopian restaurant, crying in her beer as she thumbed through the personal ads in a local newspaper.

"I was 29.9 years old with half an ovary left, and I'm freaking out looking at personal ads, thinking, 'Oh god, I just can't do it'—the same way a lot of women feel today when they go on Match.com."

Next to the personal ads, she noticed an ad for a dating agency. "I decided then and there that I'm making enough money and I'm going to hire help."

It was a fortuitous decision. The agency she hired was Great Expectations, and the St. Louis office of Great Expectations happened to be run by her future husband, Gil. The two of them hit it off immediately—so much so that Ferman kept thinking that she liked Gil way more than any of the men he was trying to set her up with.

"So one day," she says, "I knocked on his door and began flirting with him. I said, 'Hey, I didn't see your photo in the [Great Expectations client] book. What's the story?'"

"It's kind of sad," Gil replied. "I'm not supposed to ask out my members."

"Well," Ferman said, "what would happen if one of your members asked you out?"

"If she was cute, I'd probably go."

"Come on," said Ferman, "let's go grab a beer."

After three dates, Julie and Gil were inseparable. Then, two months into their relationship, Gil's parents came for a visit. His parents were staying with Gil, which meant Julie and Gil had to spend their first night apart in weeks.

"Gil drove me back to my place," Ferman reports, "and we're sitting in the driveway and he's saying to me, 'I don't like it when you're not around. I don't like it when you're not there at night. I don't like it when you're not there in the morning.'"

Ferman's playful retort: "Well, if you don't like it when I'm not around, maybe I should be around all the time."

Gil quickly got the hint. "Okay!" he said. "We'll make an announcement tomorrow when my parents are around."

"Wait a second!" Ferman replied. "We're not announcing anything to anybody until I hear the words 'I love you' and 'Will you marry me?' You've got to at least give me that!"

The next day Gil showed up on Ferman's doorstep with a bouquet of roses and a note that read, 'I do love you so let's get married.'"

Technically, Ferman didn't actually propose to Gil. What she did was the proposal equivalent of Evie's first move with Patrick in Chapter 3 (remember when Evie used her friend's phone to text, "Evie thinks you're really cute!" to Patrick?). Ferman opened the door for Gil. All Gil had to do was walk through. And *that* is Julie Ferman's definition of a feminine marriage proposal.

It's an invitation for an invitation. Your message to him: You want to spend the rest of your life with him. It's not a demand or an

It's an invitation for an invitation. Your message to him: You want to spend the rest of your life with him. It's not a demand or an ultimatum. It's an expression of love.

ultimatum. It's an expression of love. If you don't feel comfortable saying the words "Will you marry me?" (personally, I do prefer Katie's more direct approach), Ferman's "feminine marriage proposal" is surely the next best thing.

The generic version of a feminine marriage proposal might sound something like this: "I've been looking for a long time for the right person, and I love the way I feel when I'm with you. I just thought that I'd let you know I can totally envision spending the rest of my life with you."

Says Ferman, "What guy wouldn't be touched to hear that?"

And if he isn't touched? Well, that totally sucks. But it's something you need to find out—especially if you're over thirty and want to have a baby sooner rather than later. You need to know if you're wasting your time.

Last but Not Least, You Get to Pick Out Your Own Ring

Few things can sour a proposal faster than a crappy engagement ring. My own wife wasn't exactly bowled over with the simple diamond ring I got her—which is why she wound up upgrading it on her own years later. (I used to joke with her that she should consider herself lucky that I didn't buy the pear-cut, yellow-tinted diamond that the first jeweler tried to sell me.)

If your boyfriend is as fashion challenged as I was, and if the ring is important to you (and let's get real, it's important to 99.9 percent of women), that's yet another reason why you should propose to him. Once he says yes, you can go to the jewelry store together. You can pick out exactly the ring you want, and he'll be relieved that he didn't screw it up.

"No one needs a stab of disappointment every time they glance down and leftward," says Katie Burton. "Proposing is a sure fire way to get a say on the ring, and remember, you'll be wearing that thing for a ruddy long time."[20]

Join the Conversation on the
***Make Your Move* Blog at JonBirger.com**

What's the worst proposal story you've ever heard? How about the best?

CONCLUSION

For lots of you, making your move will come naturally. You're already a badass at work and at play. You're not too nervous to cold-call a venture capitalist about funding your startup or too scared to hike Angels Landing in the rain. So why the heck would you ever be afraid to ask golden retriever guy in 5E out on a date? All you needed was a little encouragement. Katie and Evie and Seleana and Tania showed you how they crushed it in today's dating market. They made their moves. Now you're ready to make yours.

Not every woman is quite so ready to make the same leap, though. A few of you are probably thinking, "But, Jon, men have it so easy already. Now you're saying women have to do the heavy lifting in dating too? It's just not fair!"

You know what? I agree. It's not fair.

If I thought the play-hard-to-get approach actually worked, I'd be all for it. So long as you're getting the guys you want, why not force men to make the first move and to jump through additional hoops along the way in order to prove their worth?

Problem is, the old rules don't work. You know that. This is not a book about how we wish the world should be. This is a book about navigating the world that is. This is a book about strategy, not philosophy. And the dating strategy that works best right now is one in which women take charge.

So put down your phone. Look up at the world around you. Every day you're brushing shoulders with single men whom you already know and like—the coworker, the neighborhood cop, the cute guy at church, maybe even an old flame. Just because these men are not on your dating app doesn't mean they shouldn't be on your dating radar. Talk to them. Learn more about them. Find out if they're single (if you don't know already). And if you still like them, do not be afraid to ask them out on dates.

Remember, men like women who like them. Remember that he wants you to make your move—no matter what your mom and your girlfriends and all those silly dating rule books have told you. While the other women sit back and wait for the right guy to find them, you are going to go out and get him first.

It's who you are. It's who more and more men are too. That guy you really like is feeling a little gun-shy these days. He's afraid of doing or saying the wrong thing. It's easier for him

> Every day you're brushing shoulders with single men whom you already know and like—the coworker, the neighborhood cop, the cute guy at church, maybe even an old flame. Just because these men are not on your dating app doesn't mean they shouldn't be on your dating radar.

to try out a line with a stranger on Tinder than it is for him to make the first move with you. He knows he may not click with Tinderella. But he thinks that as much as online dating sucks, it still sucks way less than getting embarrassed at a party or being reprimanded at work for asking out the wrong person at the wrong time.

Dating's perfect storm has arrived, and it's the perfect time for confident, successful, assertive women like you to make your move—and win.

After you've made your move, please visit the *Make Your Move* blog at JonBirger.com and post your stories—the wonderful, the terrible, and the ones with endings still unwritten. I want to hear them all. If you disagree with something written here or if I suggested something that didn't work out for you, I want to hear that too. As will other readers. You can ask me a dating question, and I'll try to answer it. And if you know the answer to someone else's question—or even if you just want to chime in with some friendly advice—the *Make Your Move* blog is the place to share it. My goal with the blog is to moderate a freewheeling conversation about postmodern dating, not to push a one-size-fits-all approach on everyone.

At the end of the day, it's still your move.

All I ask: Don't be afraid to make it a bold one.

ACKNOWLEDGMENTS

Some books practically write themselves. You've got the whole thing mapped out in your head—chapters, themes, anecdotes, and all. When it comes time to put pen to paper (or fingers to keyboard), the words just pour out like water from a pitcher.

Make Your Move was not that kind of book.

I struggled at first to find the right balance between science and storytelling. I wanted it to be lighter fare and more romantic than my last dating book, but it needed to be smart and science based too. I kept wavering on whether singles would embrace a dating book that urged them to take a break from online dating. After all, online dating is the only dating that many twenty-somethings have ever known.

Thankfully, I had a terrific support system to help me work through all the issues and concerns. Most important was my wife, Laura Grossfield Birger. Despite her very stressful, very demanding, and very high-profile job as one of the nation's top federal prosecutors—Laura is the chief of the criminal division for the US Attorney's Office for the Southern District of New York—she was always there for me as a sounding board and as a sympathetic ear. In addition to being a brilliant prosecutor, Laura also happens to be the world's finest amateur copy editor. She found time to read multiple drafts of this book, identifying countless typos and writing glitches along the way. Laura, thank you!

Next up I want to thank my literary agent, Carrie Pestritto of Laura Dail Literary Agency. Carrie believed in this book from the start (maybe even more than me at certain points!). Having an agent who is not only in my target demographic (Millennial women) but also in a mixed-collar marriage (Carrie's husband is a chef) proved to be incredibly valuable.

It's a little embarrassing when your married, middle-aged father starts writing dating books. My three sons—Alex, Eli, and Zach—probably wish I had stuck to writing about energy and investing. Nevertheless, all three of them have tolerated my midlife career change with grace and good humor. Boys, thank you. I owe extra debts of gratitude to Alex for letting me embarrass him with that high school story in Chapter 4 and also to Zach for serving as my part-time research assistant, using his college library to track down various scholarly articles for me. I'm also grateful to my parents, Barbara and Jordan Birger, for allowing me to share their story in Chapter 7.

Thank you to the entire BenBella Books team for being a true ally throughout this process. From my very first meeting with Publisher Glenn Yeffeth and Deputy Publisher Adrienne Lang in 2018, I knew BenBella would be the perfect home for me and for *Make Your Move*. My BenBella editor, Vy Tran, improved and fine-tuned the book immensely, as did copy editor Jennifer Greenstein. Art Director Sarah Avinger and her staff did a fantastic job designing the cover. Marketing

Director Jennifer Canzoneri and her associate Tanya Wardell developed a smart marketing plan and also helped me redesign the JonBirger.com website to incorporate *Make Your Move* and the *Make Your Move* blog.

I've always enjoyed talking through story and book ideas with my friend and fellow author Melanie Notkin, but Melanie deserves extra-special thanks this time around. I suck at book titles, and it was Melanie who first suggested "Make Your Move"—a title everyone at BenBella embraced from the get-go.

I'd like to thank my screen-rights agent, Randie Adler of ICM Partners, for her ongoing support and work on my behalf. Others I want to recognize for aiding me along my journey in book publishing, journalism, and media are Mel Parker, Maisie Tivnan, Hank Gilman, Bob Safian, Greg David, the late Cynthia Rigg, Andy Serwer, Tom Kearney, Eric Gelman, Denise Martin, Leigh Gallagher, and Glenn Coleman. Thank you as well to my former high school English teacher Joe Medlicott—still teaching writing in his nineties at Dartmouth College's Osher Lifelong Learning Institute—for encouraging me to pursue writing as a career many, many years ago.

Finally, thank you, thank you, thank you to all the pseudonymous women and men who shared their stories with me and their dating advice with readers. Not all their interviews made it into this book, but every one of them influenced it.

NOTES

Preface: First, a Little Backstory

1. Peter Moore, "Young Americans Are Less Wedded to Monogamy Than Their Elders," YouGov, October 3, 2016, https://today.yougov.com /topics/lifestyle/articles-reports/2016/10/03/young-americans-less -wedded-monogamy.
2. Irène Némirovsky, *The Fires of Autumn* (New York: Vintage, 2015), 107.
3. Marcia Guttentag and Paul F. Secord, *Too Many Women? The Sex Ratio Question* (Beverly Hills, CA: Sage, 1983), 191, 195.

Chapter 1: Breaking the Rules

1. *The Great Love Debate*, https://www.greatlovedebate.com/.
2. Katie Way, "I Went on a Date with Aziz Ansari. It Turned into the Worst Night of My Life," Babe, January 13, 2018, https://babe.net /2018/01/13/aziz-ansari-28355.
3. *Cambridge Advanced Learner's Dictionary & Thesaurus*, s.v. "play hard to get," https://dictionary.cambridge.org/us/dictionary/english/play-hard -to-get.
4. Ellen Fein and Sherrie Schneider, *The Rules: Time-Tested Secrets for Capturing the Heart of Mr. Right* (1995; repr., New York: Grand Central, 2001), 8.

5. Ellen Fein and Sherrie Schneider, *Not Your Mother's Rules: The New Secrets of Dating* (New York: Grand Central, 2013), 5.

6. Sherry Argov, *Why Men Love Bitches: From Doormat to Dreamgirl—a Woman's Guide to Holding Her Own in a Relationship* (New York: Adams Media, 2002), 44.

7. Leslie Braswell, *Ignore the Guy, Get the Guy: The Art of No Contact: A Woman's Survival Guide to Mastering a Breakup and Taking Back Her Power* (Scotts Valley, CA: CreateSpace, 2013), 85.

8. Kara King, *The Power of the Pussy: How to Get What You Want from Men: Love, Respect, Commitment and More!* (Scotts Valley, CA: CreateSpace, 2012), 99.

9. Anna North, "How Self-Help Books Hurt Women," *Jezebel*, June 15, 2009, https://jezebel.com/how-self-help-books-hurt-women-5291177.

10. Kim Knight, "Has the #MeToo Movement Killed Flirting?," *NZ Herald*, March 3, 2018, https://www.nzherald.co.nz/lifestyle/news/article.cfm?c_id=6&objectid=12004410.

11. Lisa Bonos, "'It's Tough for Me to Know Where the Line Is': The #MeToo Era Is Making Dating More Confusing," *Washington Post*, February 12, 2018, https://www.washingtonpost.com/news/soloish/wp/2018/02/12/its-tough-for-me-to-know-where-the-line-is-the-metoo-era-is-making-dating-more-confusing/.

12. Hannah Gale, "The Average Tinder User Spends an Hour and a Half a Day Swiping on the App, Oh You Guys," *Metro*, October 31, 2014, https://metro.co.uk/2014/10/31/the-average-tinder-user-spends-an-hour-and-a-half-a-day-swiping-on-the-app-oh-you-guys-4929887/.

13. Stephen Florival, "Girl Asks Twitter for Help to Find Guy Sitting Behind Her at Tennessee Football Game, Twitter Declines Hilariously and Discovers She's Tried to Use Twitter to Find Love Before (Tweets)," *Black Sports Online*, October 11, 2019, https://blacksportsonline.com/2019/10/girl-asks-twitter-for-help-to-find-guy-sitting-behind-her-at-tennessee-football-game-twitter-declines-hilariously-and-discovers-shes-tried-to-use-twitter-to-find-love-before-tweets/.

14. Corinne Purtill, "Internet Dating Is Killing the Workplace Romance," Yahoo! Finance, February 19, 2019, https://finance.yahoo.com/news/internet-dating-killing-workplace-romance-110040347.html.

15. Fein and Schneider, *The Rules*, 64.

16. "Singles Survey Finds More Men Want Women to Make First Move," CBS News, February 14, 2017, https://www.cbsnews.com/news/survey-of-singles-in-america-match-com-helen-fisher/.

17. "Women in the Labor Force: A Databook," BLS Reports, US Bureau of Labor Statistics, November 2017, https://www.bls.gov/opub/reports/womens-databook/2017/home.htm.

18. Richard Fry and D'Vera Cohn, "Women, Men and the New Economics of Marriage," Pew Research Center, January 19, 2010, https://www.pewsocialtrends.org/2010/01/19/women-men-and-the-new-economics-of-marriage/.

19. Jon Birger, "Why Getting into Elite Colleges Is Harder for Women," *Washington Post*, July 30, 2015, https://www.washingtonpost.com/posteverything/wp/2015/07/30/achieving-perfect-gender-balance-on-campus-isnt-that-important-ending-private-colleges-affirmative-action-for-men-is/.

20. Eric Planin, "Data Shows Millennial Women Are Dominating the Current Job Market," *Inc.*, May 23, 2017, https://www.inc.com/the-fiscal-times/millennial-women-dominate-job-market-men-overshadowed.html.

21. Katie Johnston, "Young Men Falling to the Bottom of the Income Ladder," *Boston Globe*, May 22, 2017, https://www3.bostonglobe.com/business/2017/05/21/young-men-falling-bottom-income-ladder/ncYhOoItuoqdlApn6qZRSL/story.html.

22. Clare O'Connor, "Men Offered Higher Pay Than Women for Same Job 69% of Time, Study Shows," *Forbes*, April 12, 2016, https://www.forbes.com/sites/clareoconnor/2016/04/12/men-offered-higher-pay-than-women-for-same-job-69-of-time-study-shows/#1d12ef0756bb.

Chapter 2: Suitor's Advantage

1. Huomenna, "Guys of Reddit, What's the Most Obvious 'Hint' from a Girl You've Missed?," *Reddit*, September 24, 2016, https://www.reddit .com/r/AskReddit/comments/54b7xx/guys_of_reddit_whats_the _most_obvious_hint_from_a/.

2. Christine Metz Howard, "Flirting Hard to Detect, Researcher Says," University of Kansas, June 4, 2014, https://news.ku.edu/2014/06/03 /flirting-hard-detect-study-finds.

3. Alvin E. Roth and Lloyd S. Shapley, "Stable Matching: Theory, Evidence, and Practical Design," Royal Swedish Academy of Sciences, 2012, https://www.nobelprize.org/uploads/2018/06/popular -economicsciences2012.pdf.

4. David Gale and Lloyd S. Shapley, "College Admissions and the Stability of Marriage," Technical Report No. 1, 1960–61, Prepared Under Contract Nonr-562(15) for the Logistics Branch of the Office of Naval Research, https://apps.dtic.mil/dtic/tr/fulltext/u2/251958.pdf.

5. "A Woman's Advantage," OkCupid, March 5, 2015, https://theblog .okcupid.com/a-womans-advantage-82d5074dde2d.

6. "OkCupid Data Finds Women Who Make First Move Online Have Better Results," ABC News, March 20, 2016, https://abcnews.go.com /Lifestyle/okcupid-data-finds-women-make-move-online-results /story?id=37536624.

7. Tim Teeman, "18 Years Ago She Wrote the Rules of Dating. But Are They Relevant Now?," *Times* (London), January 16, 2013, http://www .timteeman.com/2013/01/16/18-years-ago-she-wrote-the-rules-of -dating-but-are-they-relevant-now/.

8. Angela Saini, *Inferior: How Science Got Women Wrong—and the New Research That's Rewriting the Story* (Boston: Beacon Press, 2018), 143.

9. Scott Jaschik, "Some Professors Defend Ties to Financier Accused of Using Underage Girls," *Inside Higher Ed*, February 2, 2015, https:// www.insidehighered.com/quicktakes/2015/02/02/some-professors -defend-ties-financier-accused-using-underage-girls.

10. Jennifer C. D. MacGregor and Justin V. Cavallo, "Breaking the Rules: Personal Control Increases Women's Direct Relationship Initiation," *Journal of Social and Personal Relationships* 28, no. 6 (2011): 848–67, https://journals.sagepub.com/doi/pdf/10.1177/0265407510397986.

11. Saini, *Inferior*, 123.

12. Saini, *Inferior*, 124.

13. Saini, *Inferior*, 127.

14. Saini, *Inferior*, 135.

15. Saini, *Inferior*, 128.

16. Rukmini Callimachi, "Women, Not Men, Choose Spouses on African Archipelago," *USA Today*, February 3, 2007, https://usatoday30.usatoday.com/news/world/2007-02-02-ladies-choice_x.htm.

17. "Where Women Propose and Men Can't Say No," CBS News, February 1, 2007, https://www.cbsnews.com/news/where-women-propose-and-men-cant-say-no/.

18. "Africa's Most Original Culture Where Women Rule Their World," *VozAfric*, February 7, 2015, https://www.vozafric.com/africas-most-original-culture-where-women-rule-their-world/.

19. Sari M. van Anders, Jeffrey Steiger, and Katherine L. Goldey, "Effects of Gendered Behavior on Testosterone in Women and Men," *Proceedings of the National Academy of Sciences* 112, no. 45 (2015): 13805–10, https://www.pnas.org/content/112/45/13805.

20. Thomas G. Travison, Andre B. Araujo, Amy B. O'Donnell, Varant Kupelian, and John B. McKinlay, "A Population-Level Decline in Serum Testosterone Levels in American Men," *Journal of Clinical Endocrinology & Metabolism* 92, no. 1 (2007), 196–202, https://academic.oup.com/jcem/article/92/1/196/2598434.

21. William J. Cromie, "Marriage Lowers Testosterone," *Harvard Gazette*, August 22, 2002, https://news.harvard.edu/gazette/story/2002/08/marriage-lowers-testosterone/.

22. David French, "Men Are Getting Weaker—Because We're Not Raising Men," *National Review*, August 16, 2016, https://www.nationalreview.com/2016/08/male-physical-decline-masculinity-threatened/.

23. "Ann Coulter on REAL MEN, Trump, and the Feminization of America (Excerpt 3 of 3)," YouTube video, 4:25, posted by "The Fallen State," April 29, 2017, https://www.youtube.com/watch?v=FeK5nFc_5h0.

24. Chimamanda Ngozi Adichie, *We Should All Be Feminists* (New York: Anchor Books, 2015), 26.

25. Jeremy Beaman, "Male College Students to Undergo 'Critical Self-Reflection' of Masculinity," *The College Fix*, January 3, 2017, https://www.thecollegefix.com/male-college-students-undergo-critical-self-reflection-masculinity/.

26. Alissa Lopez, "Students Told Term 'Be a Man' Represents Toxic Masculinity," *The College Fix*, October 18, 2016, https://www.thecollegefix.com/students-told-term-man-represents-toxic-masculinity/.

27. Pelin Gul and Tom R. Kupfer, "Benevolent Sexism and Mate Preferences: Why Do Women Prefer Benevolent Men Despite Recognizing That They Can Be Undermining?," *Personality and Social Psychology Bulletin*, June 29, 2018, https://journals.sagepub.com/doi/abs/10.1177/0146167218781000?journalCode=pspc.

28. Dixie Laite, "My Perverted Feelings for Mr. Rogers," *Dametown*, April 8, 2013, https://www.dametown.com/my-perverted-feelings-for-mr-rogers/.

29. "John Wayne Spanks Elizabeth Allen," YouTube video, 0:28, posted by "MrBdub14," March 31, 2010, https://www.youtube.com/watch?v=50_JqltsgPM.

30. "The Quiet Man" (kiss scene), YouTube video, 2:35, posted by "Secchiaroli," July 29, 2014, https://www.youtube.com/watch?v=MkQyRE0byBI.

31. Michelle Trudeau, "Human Connections Start with a Friendly Touch," NPR, September 20, 2010, https://www.npr.org/templates/story/story.php?storyId=128795325.

32. Duana C. Welch, "Stolen Kisses: Why We Don't Want to Be Asked First, but You'd Better Ask Our Kids," *Love Science*, February 20, 2013, http://www.lovesciencemedia.com/love-science-media/stolen-kisses-why-we-dont-want-to-be-asked-first-but-youd-be.html.

Chapter 3: Men Like Women Who Like Them

1. Fein and Schneider, *The Rules*, 88.
2. Argov, *Why Men Love Bitches*, 96.
3. "How to Make a Feminist Dating App," *Atlantic* video, 4:41, November 1, 2016, https://www.theatlantic.com/video/index/506036/whitney -wolfe-bumble/.
4. "Bumble Super Bowl Commercial 2019 with Serena Williams," Daily-Motion video, 1:00, posted by "Fan Reviews," February 3, 2019, https://www.dailymotion.com/video/x71rnu4.
5. Darla Murray, "What 12 Women Learned from Making the First Move," *Elle*, March 9, 2017, https://www.elle.com/life-love/sex -relationships/g29612/why-its-good-to-make-the-first-move/.
6. "Do More Than Say Hi," *Messy Mentor*, May 15, 2018, http://messy mentor.strikingly.com/blog/do-more-than-say-hi (site discontinued).
7. Lisa Zhang, comment on "A Girl Rolls Her Eyes When I Say 'Hi'?," *Girls Ask Guys*, September 25, 2014, https://www.girlsaskguys.com/ girls-behavior/q1156417-a-girl-rolls-her-eyes-when-i-say-hi.
8. Jeremy Nicholson, "Just Ask for It! Part I," *Psychology Today*, May 13, 2011, https://www.psychologytoday.com/us/blog/the-attraction -doctor/201105/just-asking-it-part-i.
9. Shari L. Dworkin and Lucia O'Sullivan, "Actual Versus Desired Initiation Patterns Among a Sample of College Men: Tapping Disjunctures Within Traditional Male Sexual Scripts," *Journal of Sex Research* 42, no. 2 (2005): 150–8, https://www.researchgate.net/publication/7636542 _Actual_versus_desired_initiation_patterns_among_a_sample_of _college_men_Tapping_disjunctures_within_traditional_male_sexual _scripts.
10. John Tierney, "A Cold War Fought by Women," *New York Times*, November 18, 2013, https://www.nytimes.com/2013/11/19/science/a -cold-war-fought-by-women.html.

11. Tracy Vaillancourt and Aanchal Sharma, "Intolerance of Sexy Peers: Intrasexual Competition Among Women," *Aggressive Behavior* 37 (2011): 569–77, http://awmueller.com/psicologia/intolerance.pdf.

Chapter 4: Date Who You Know

1. Jon Gitlin, "Dating Apps Are Common, Useful—and Widely Disliked," SurveyMonkey, April 30, 2018, https://www.surveymonkey .com/curiosity/dating-apps-and-sites-are-almost-as-common-as-they -are-disliked/.

2. Monica Anderson, Emily A. Vogels, and Erica Turner, "The Virtues and Downsides of Online Dating," Pew Research Center, February 6, 2020, https://www.pewresearch.org/internet/2020/02/06/the-virtues -and-downsides-of-online-dating/.

3. Peter Lynch with John Rothchild, *One Up On Wall Street: How to Use What You Already Know to Make Money in the Market* (New York: Simon & Schuster, 2000), 100–101.

4. Helen Fisher, "How Coronavirus Is Changing the Dating Game for the Better," *New York Times*, May 7, 2020, https://www.nytimes.com/2020 /05/07/well/mind/dating-coronavirus-love-relationships.html.

5. Ed Tobias, "Checking Out a Dating App for People with Health Problems," *Multiple Sclerosis News Today*, August 31, 2018, https://multiple sclerosisnewstoday.com/2018/08/31/ms-lemonayde-dating-app-people -health-problems/.

6. Bonnie Rochman, "A New Dating Site for People Who Can't Have Sex," *Time*, August 18, 2011, https://healthland.time.com/2011/08/18 /dating-site-for-people-who-cant-have-sex-takes-off/.

7. Match Group, "Annual Report Pursuant to Section 13 or 15(d) of the Securities Exchange Act of 1934," United States Securities and Exchange Commission, filed on February 28, 2019, https://www.sec .gov/Archives/edgar/data/1575189/000157518919000020/mtch10 -k20181231.htm.

8. Match Group, "Match Group, Inc. Report on Form 10-K for the Fiscal Year Ended December 31, 2018," United States Securities and Exchange Commission, filed on February 28, 2019, https://s22.q4cdn .com/279430125/files/doc_financials/2018/annual/Match-Group -2018-Annual-Report-to-Stockholders_vF.pdf.

9. Aditi Paul, "Is Online Better Than Offline for Meeting Partners? Depends: Are You Looking to Marry or to Date?," *Cyberpsychology, Behavior, and Social Networking* 17, no. 10 (2014), https://www .researchgate.net/publication/265692811_Is_Online_Better_Than _Offline_for_Meeting_Partners_Depends_Are_You_Looking_to _Marry_or_to_Date.

10. Michael J. Rosenfeld and Reuben J. Thomas, "Searching for a Mate: The Rise of the Internet as a Social Intermediary," *American Sociological Review* 77, no. 4 (2012), 523–547.

11. John T. Cacioppo, Stephanie Cacioppo, et al., "Marital Satisfaction and Break-Ups Differ Across On-Line and Off-Line Meeting Venues," *Proceedings of the National Academy of Sciences* 110, no. 25 (2013), https:// www.researchgate.net/publication/237018069_Marital_satisfaction _and_break-ups_differ_across_on-line_and_off-line_meeting_venues.

12. James O'Toole, "OkCupid Set Up Bad Dates in 'an Experiment,'" CNN Business, July 28, 2014, https://money.cnn.com/2014/07/28 /technology/social/okcupid-experiment/index.html.

13. Susan Sprecher and Adam J. Hampton, "Liking and Other Reactions After a Get-Acquainted Interaction: A Comparison of Continuous Face-to-Face Interaction Versus Interaction That Progresses from Text Messages to Face-to-Face," *Communications Quarterly* 65, no. 3 (2017), https://www.tandfonline.com/doi/abs/10.1080/01463373.2016 .1256334?src=recsys&journalCode=rcqu20.

14. Julia Sklar, "'Zoom Fatigue' Is Taxing the Brain. Here's Why That Happens," *National Geographic*, April 24, 2020, https://www.national geographic.com/science/2020/04/coronavirus-zoom-fatigue-is-taxing -the-brain-here-is-why-that-happens/#close.

15. Miranda Levy, "I Found a Boyfriend Online in My 50s—But I Don't Want to Meet Him," *Telegraph*, August 7, 2019, https://www.telegraph.co.uk/women/sex/found-boyfriend-online-50s-dont-want-meet/.

16. Sharon Sassler and Amanda Jayne Miller, "The Ecology of Relationships: Meeting Locations and Cohabitors' Relationship Perceptions," *Journal of Social and Personal Relationships* 32, no. 2 (2015), https://journals.sagepub.com/doi/full/10.1177/0265407514525886.

17. Taylor Ferber, "Kate Beckinsale Reflects on 'Serendipity' 15 Years Later—Is She Still a Sucker for Fate?," *Bustle*, May 16, 2016, https://www.bustle.com/articles/160680-kate-beckinsale-reflects-on-serendipity-15-years-later-is-she-still-a-sucker-for-fate.

18. Nicole Alea and Stephanie C. Vick, "The First Sight of Love: Relationship-Defining Memories and Marital Satisfaction Across Adulthood," *Memory* 18, no. 7 (2010): 730–42, https://www.researchgate.net/publication/45709791_The_first_sight_of_love_Relationship-defining_memories_and_marital_satisfaction_across_adulthood.

19. Zoe McKnight, "Online Dating Shaking Up the Meet-Cute," *Toronto Star*, November 13, 2017, https://www.thestar.com/life/relationships/2017/11/13/online-dating-shaking-up-the-meet-cute.html.

20. Philip Alan Belove, "How Love Writes Its Truths on Your Soul, and How You Can Read What It Has Written," *How Relationships Work*, July 22, 2014, https://www.drbelove.com/how-love-writes-its-truths-on-your-soul-and-how-you-can-read-what-it-has-written/ (site discontinued).

21. Paul, "Is Online Better Than Offline for Meeting Partners?"

22. Paul Hiebert, "The Paradox of Choice, 10 Years Later," *Pacific Standard*, published December 18, 2014, updated June 14, 2017, https://psmag.com/social-justice/paradox-choice-barry-schwartz-psychology-10-years-later-96706.

23. Käri Knutson, "Online Dating Study Shows Too Many Choices Can Lead to Dissatisfaction," University of Wisconsin–Madison, June 13, 2017, https://news.wisc.edu/online-dating-study-shows-too-many-choices-can-lead-to-dissatisfaction/.

24. Paul, "Is Online Better Than Offline for Meeting Partners?"

Chapter 5: The Make Your Move Offline Dating Challenge

1. Eimear O'Hagan, "Dating Detox: I Gave Up on Men After 10 Years of Online Dating . . . Then I Met Mr Right," *Sun*, March 29, 2020, https://www.thesun.co.uk/fabulous/11264583/gave-up-online-dating-mr-right/.

2. Zahra Barnes, "9 Types of Guys You'll Meet Online," *Glamour*, November 6, 2014, https://www.glamour.com/story/9-types-of-guys-youll-meet-onl.

3. O'Hagan, "Dating Detox."

4. Giedrè Vaičiulaitytė, "Women Are Sharing the Responses They Got After Asking Out Their Crush on a Date, and It's Too Entertaining," *Bored Panda*, October 26, 2017, https://www.boredpanda.com/oloni-girls-ask-guys-datechallenge-responses-twitter/.

5. Brené Brown, *Daring Greatly: How the Courage to Be Vulnerable Transforms the Way We Live, Love, Parent, and Lead* (New York: Avery, 2012), 42.

6. Anna Bruk, Sabine G. Scholl, and Herbert Bless, "Beautiful Mess Effect: Self-Other Differences in Evaluation of Showing Vulnerability," *Journal of Personality and Social Psychology* 115, no. 2 (2018): 192–205, https://www.researchgate.net/publication/326743464_Beautiful_mess_effect_Self-other_differences_in_evaluation_of_showing_vulnerability.

Chapter 6: Long Live the Office Romance

1. Adrian Furnham, "On Your Head: Don't Be Surprised to Find Cupid Among the Cubicles," *Times* (London), February 12, 2012, https://www.thetimes.co.uk/article/on-your-head-dont-be-surprised-to-find-cupid-among-the-cubicles-5rq2mdnvs2p.

2. "Office Romance Hits 10-Year Low, According to CareerBuilder's Annual Valentine's Day Survey," CareerBuilder, February 1, 2018, http://press.careerbuilder.com/2018-02-01-Office-Romance-Hits-10-Year-Low-According-to-CareerBuilders-Annual-Valentines-Day-Survey.

3. Ruth Styles, "Looking for Love? Try the Office! Relationships That Begin in the Workplace Most Likely to Result in Marriage," *Daily Mail*, September 29, 2013, https://www.dailymail.co.uk/femail/article -2437181/Relationships-begin-workplace-likely-result-marriage-new -study-reveals.html.

4. Furnham, "On Your Head: Don't Be Surprised to Find Cupid Among the Cubicles."

5. Stephanie Losee and Helaine Olen, *Office Mate: The Employee Handbook for Finding—and Managing—Romance on the Job* (Avon, MA: Adams Media, 2007), 18.

6. "Survey Finds Employment Background Checks Nearly Universal Today," Global HR Research, https://www.ghrr.com/survey-finds -employment-background-checks-nearly-universal-today/.

7. Corinne Purtill and Dan Kopf, "Internet Dating Is Killing the Workplace Romance," *Quartz at Work*, February 19, 2019, https://qz.com /work/1552337/workplace-dating-is-declining/.

8. Angela B. Cummings, "Workplace Romances: Do They 'Suit' Your Company?," *Mondaq*, November 14, 2017, http://www.mondaq.com /unitedstates/x/645908/employee+rights+labour+relations/Workplace +Romances+Do+They+Suit+Your+Company.

9. James A. Gagliano, "How to Date in 2018," CNN Opinion, January 22, 2018, https://www.cnn.com/2018/01/21/opinions/how-to-date-in -2018-opinion-roundup/index.html.

10. "The 2018 Vault Office Romance Survey Results," Vault, February 12, 2018, https://www.vault.com/blogs/workplace-issues/2018-vault -office-romance-survey-results.

11. Simon Goodley, "American Apparel Bans Work Romances," *Guardian*, January 7, 2015, https://www.theguardian.com/business/2015/jan/07 /american-apparel-bans-work-romances.

12. Cathy Bussewitz and Dee-Ann Durbin, "McDonald's CEO Pushed Out After Relationship with Employee," AP News, November 3, 2019, https://apnews.com/7b8aa56cb9194edc8802093085f4c254.

13. Susan Matthews, "The Quiet Radicalism of Facebook and Google's Dating Policy," *Slate*, February 6, 2018, https://slate.com/technology/2018/02/google-and-facebooks-dating-policies-are-quietly-radical.html.

14. "Melinda Gates, Co-chair and Trustee, Bill & Melinda Gates Foundation," *Makers* video, 5:37, August 20, 2019, https://www.yahoo.com/lifestyle/melinda-gates-co-chair-trustee-233312756.html.

Chapter 7: Get 'Em While You're Young—or They Are!

1. Meg Jay, *The Defining Decade: Why Your Twenties Matter—and How to Make the Most of Them Now* (New York: Twelve, 2012), xxii.

2. Jay, *The Defining Decade*, xxiii.

3. "Sex by Age by Educational Attainment for the Population 18 Years and Over," United States Census Bureau, https://data.census.gov/cedsci/table?g=0500000US06037,11001,12086&tid=ACSDT1Y2017.B15001&q=B15001.

4. "School Enrollment, Tertiary (Gross), Gender Parity Index (GPI)," UNESCO Institute for Statistics, https://data.worldbank.org/indicator/SE.ENR.TERT.FM.ZS?end=2011&name_desc=false&start=1970.

5. Ellen Nguyen, "Why You Should Choose Career Over Relationships in Your Early 20s," Tingly Mind, May 24, 2015, http://www.tinglymind.com/career-or-relationships/.

6. Beca Grimm, "7 Reasons Why People Who Prioritize Career Over Romantic Relationships Are Happier—and More Successful," *Bustle*, January 6, 2015, https://www.bustle.com/articles/56985-7-reasons-why-people-who-prioritize-career-over-romantic-relationships-are-happier-and-more-successful.

7. Joseph Price, "Does a Spouse Slow You Down? Marriage and Graduate Student Outcomes," Cornell University, https://archive.ilr.cornell.edu/sites/default/files/WP94.pdf.

8. Alexandra Killewald and Margaret Gough, "Does Specialization Explain Marriage Penalties and Premiums?," *American Sociological*

Review 78, no. 3 (2013): 477–502, https://www.ncbi.nlm.nih.gov/pmc /articles/PMC3769138/.

9. Joseph Chamie, "Out-of-Wedlock Births Rise Worldwide," *YaleGlobal Online*, March 16, 2017, https://yaleglobal.yale.edu/content/out -wedlock-births-rise-worldwide.

10. Killewald and Gough, "Does Specialization Explain Marriage Penalties and Premiums?"

11. Killewald and Gough, "Does Specialization Explain Marriage Penalties and Premiums?"

12. Lisa Arnold and Christina Campbell, "The High Price of Being Single in America," *Atlantic*, January 14, 2013, https://www.theatlantic.com/sexes /archive/2013/01/the-high-price-of-being-single-in-america/267043/.

13. "Most Powerful Women," *Fortune*, 2019, https://fortune.com/most -powerful-women/.

14. Kristine Fellizar, "Millennials Spend an Average of 10 Hours a Week on Dating Apps, Survey Finds, but Here's What Experts Actually Recommend," *Bustle*, January 31, 2018, https://www.bustle.com/p /millennials-spend-average-of-10-hours-a-week-on-dating-apps-survey -finds-but-heres-what-experts-actually-recommend-8066805.

15. Queensland University of Technology, "Women Know What They Want; Men Get Pickier with Age," *ScienceDaily*, June 26, 2018, https:// www.sciencedaily.com/releases/2018/06/180626113412.htm.

16. Rachel Thorpe et al., "Sex and the (Older) Single Girl: Experiences of Sex and Dating in Later Life," *Journal of Aging Studies*, 2015, https://www.academia.edu/17444653/Sex_and_the_older_single_girl _Experiences_of_sex_and_dating_in_later_life.

17. Lisa Schuman, https://www.rmact.com/integrated-fertility-and-wellness -team/lisa-schuman.

18. Dale Markowitz, "Undressed: What's the Deal with the Age Gap in Relationships?," OkCupid, June 1, 2017, https://theblog.okcupid .com/undressed-whats-the-deal-with-the-age-gap-in-relationships -3143a2ca5178.

19. "America's Families and Living Arrangements: 2017," United States Census Bureau, 2017, https://www.census.gov/data/tables/2017/demo /families/cps-2017.html.

20. Carol Morello, "Number of Long-Lasting Marriages in U.S. Has Risen, Census Bureau Reports," *Washington Post*, May 18, 2011, https://www .washingtonpost.com/local/number-of-long-lasting-marriages-in-us -has-risen-census-bureau-reports/2011/05/18/AFO8dW6G_story .html?noredirect=on&utm_term=.76e30a2f4fd1.

21. Markowitz, "Undressed: What's the Deal with the Age Gap in Relationships?"

22. "Live Births and Birth Rates, by Year," Infoplease, https://www.info please.com/us/births/live-births-and-birth-rates-year.

23. Guttentag and Secord, *Too Many Women?*

24. "Bachelor's Degrees Conferred by Postsecondary Institutions, by Race/ Ethnicity and Sex of Student: Selected Years, 1976–77 Through 2017– 18," National Center for Education Statistics, https://nces.ed.gov /programs/digest/d19/tables/dt19_322.20.asp.

25. Jenna Birch, "Why Are Men Still So Afraid of Ambitious Women?," *Cosmopolitan*, June 13, 2017, https://www.cosmopolitan.com/sex-love /a10000998/ambition-and-dating/.

26. Markowitz, "Undressed: What's the Deal with the Age Gap in Relationships?"

27. "The Case for an Older Woman," OkCupid, February 16, 2010, https:// theblog.okcupid.com/the-case-for-an-older-woman-99d8cabacdf5.

Chapter 8: Second Time Is a Charm

1. "Historical Marital Status Tables," United States Census Bureau, November 2019, https://www.census.gov/data/tables/time-series/demo /families/marital.html.

2. Olivia Goldhill, "The Psychology of Why Rekindled Romances Are So Intense," *Quartz*, December 20, 2015, https://qz.com/578395/the -psychology-of-why-rekindled-romances-are-so-intense/.

3. Goldhill, "The Psychology of Why Rekindled Romances Are So Intense."

4. Shirley Glass with Jean Coppock Staeheli, *NOT "Just Friends": Rebuilding Trust and Recovering Your Sanity After Infidelity* (New York: Free Press, 2003), 9.

5. Joanne Laucius, "First Love: Ever Wonder What Happened to the Love You Left Behind?," Canada.com, February 11, 2011, http://www.canada.com/life/first+love+ever+wonder+what+happened+love+left+behind/4267552/story.html.

Chapter 9: Uncheck the College Box

1. Tashara Jones, "Lori Stokes Can't Find a Date," Page Six, February 26, 2018, https://pagesix.com/2018/02/26/lori-stokes-cant-find-a-date/.

2. Emine Saner, "The Dating Gap: Why the Odds Are Stacked Against Female Graduates Finding a Like-Minded Man," *Guardian*, November 10, 2015, https://www.theguardian.com/lifeandstyle/2015/nov/10/dating-gap-hook-up-culture-female-graduates.

3. "Married-Couple Families with Wives' Earnings Greater Than Husbands' Earnings: 1981 to 2018," US Bureau of the Census, Current Population Survey, Annual Social and Economic Supplements, https://www2.census.gov/programs-surveys/cps/tables/time-series/historical-income-families/f22.xls.

4. Marta Murray-Close and Misty L. Heggeness, "Manning Up and Womaning Down: How Husbands and Wives Report Their Earnings When She Earns More," US Census Bureau, June 6, 2018, https://www.census.gov/library/working-papers/2018/demo/SEHSD-WP2018-20.html.

5. Fry and Cohn, "Women, Men and the New Economics of Marriage."

6. Blixa Scott, "Why I Love My Blue-Collar Guy," The Good Men Project, November 1, 2018, https://goodmenproject.com/featured-content/why-i-love-my-blue-collar-guy/.

7. Anna Davies, "The Solution to NYC's Man Drought? Date Down," *New York Post*, June 1, 2016, https://nypost.com/2016/06/01/the-solution-to-nycs-man-drought-date-down/.

8. Kendra Bischoff and Sean F. Reardon, "Residential Segregation by Income, 1970–2009," Brown University, October 16, 2013, https://s4.ad.brown.edu/Projects/Diversity/Data/Report/report10162013.pdf.

9. Jan Van Bavel, Christine R. Schwarz, and Albert Esteve, "The Reversal of the Gender Gap in Education and Its Consequences for Family Life," *Annual Review of Sociology* 44 (2018): 341–60, https://www.annualreviews.org/doi/abs/10.1146/annurev-soc-073117-041215.

10. Kacie McCoy, "6 Interesting Stats About Infidelity in the United States," *SheKnows*, October 16, 2015, https://www.sheknows.com/health-and-wellness/articles/1094819/cheating-stats-in-america/.

11. Jennifer L. S. Weber, Twitter post, September 14, 2015, 2:58 AM, https://twitter.com/allthingsjen/status/643363204773609472.

12. Stephanie Rosenbloom, "Mr. Right, It Turns Out, Does Not Take Classes," *New York Times*, May 17, 2007, https://www.nytimes.com/2007/05/17/fashion/17Dating.html.

13. "Marriages in the Last Year by Sex by Marital Status for the Population 15 Years and Over," United States Census Bureau, https://data.census.gov/cedsci/table?g=0400000US39&tid=ACSDT1Y2016.B12501&q=B12501.

14. Seleana Bines, "How I Realized It Was Okay to Date a Man Less Educated Than I Am," *Washington Post*, July 20, 2017, https://www.washingtonpost.com/news/soloish/wp/2017/07/20/how-i-realized-it-was-okay-to-date-a-man-less-educated-than-i-am/.

Chapter 10: The Reluctant Groom

1. Lane Moore, "New Data Shows an Insane Number of Women Have Turned Down Marriage Proposals," *Cosmopolitan*, February 10, 2015, https://www.cosmopolitan.com/sex-love/news/a36313/new-data

-shows-an-insane-number-of-women-have-turned-down-marriage
-proposals/.

2. Lucia Peters, "Rejected Marriage Proposals: The Top 5 Reasons People Say 'No' to Getting Engaged," *Bustle*, October 30, 2014, https://www.bustle.com/articles/46763-rejected-marriage-proposals-the-top-5-reasons-people-say-no-to-getting-engaged.

3. David Schweingruber, Alicia D. Cast, and Sine Anahita, "'A Story and a Ring': Audience Judgments About Engagement Proposals," *Sex Roles* 58, no. 3–4 (2008): 165–78, https://link.springer.com/article/10.1007/s11199-007-9330-1.

4. Katie Burton, "I Will Never Regret Proposing to My Boyfriend—More Women Should Pop the Question," *HuffPost UK*, December 2, 2018, https://www.huffingtonpost.co.uk/entry/why-women-should-propose_uk_5a81734de4b033149e401d4a.

5. Peter Gray, "How Hunter-Gatherers Maintained Their Egalitarian Ways," *Psychology Today*, May 16, 2011, https://www.psychologytoday.com/us/blog/freedom-learn/201105/how-hunter-gatherers-maintained-their-egalitarian-ways.

6. Michael Luo, "'Excuse Me. May I Have Your Seat?,'" *New York Times*, September 14, 2004, https://www.nytimes.com/2004/09/14/nyregion/excuse-me-may-i-have-your-seat.html.

7. Julia Stuart, "Excuse Me, Can I Have Your Seat, Please?," *Independent*, September 22, 2004, https://www.independent.co.uk/news/uk/this-britain/excuse-me-can-i-have-your-seat-please-547159.html.

8. Jake, "Does He Want You to Propose?," *Glamour*, May 19, 2015, https://www.glamour.com/story/women-proposing-to-men-first.

9. Reuters, "He Said Yes! 73% of British Men to Say Yes If Partner Proposed," *Daily Mail*, February 15, 2016, https://www.dailymail.co.uk/wires/reuters/article-3447850/He-Said-Yes-73-British-Men-To-Say-Yes-Partner-Proposed.html.

10. Stephanie Coontz, *Marriage, a History: How Love Conquered Marriage* (New York: Penguin Books, 2006).

11. Amy Coombs, "Why Don't Women Propose?," *GoodTimes*, February 12, 2013, http://goodtimes.sc/uncategorized/why-dont-women-propose/.

12. Burton, "I Will Never Regret Proposing to My Boyfriend."

13. Elizabeth Warren, Facebook post, July 12, 2016, https://www.facebook .com/ElizabethWarren/posts/i-proposed-to-bruce-in-a-classroom-it -was-the-first-time-id-seen-him-teach-and-i/10153894305058687/.

14. "Lorraine Proposes to Her Man Live on Air," *Eastbourne Herald*, March 4, 2008, https://www.eastbourneherald.co.uk/news/lorraine-proposes -to-her-man-live-on-air-1-1416934.

15. Miles Godfrey, "Leap Year Wedding for Competition Couple," *Argus*, February 29, 2008, https://www.theargus.co.uk/news/2085014.amp/.

16. Tauriq Moosa, "Public Marriage Proposals Must Die," *Daily Beast*, April 14, 2017, https://www.thedailybeast.com/public-marriage-proposals -must-die.

17. Shannon Proudfoot, "Let's Just Be Honest, Public Proposals Are NOT Romantic," *Flare*, January 11, 2019, https://www.flare.com/sex-and -relationships/public-proposal/.

18. Stephanie Kaloi, "Proposing in Public Is the Worst and You Should Never Do It," A Practical Wedding, published September 21, 2016, updated October 27, 2017, https://apracticalwedding.com/proposing -in-public/.

19. Dean Burnett, "Public Proposals: True Romance or Unwarranted Coercion?," *Guardian*, August 16, 2016, https://www.theguardian.com /science/brain-flapping/2016/aug/16/public-proposals-true-romance -or-unwarranted-coercion-olympic-podium-proposal.

20. Burton, "I Will Never Regret Proposing to My Boyfriend."

ABOUT THE AUTHOR

Photo by Nicole Engelmann

JON BIRGER is an award-winning magazine writer, *Fortune* contributor, and author of *Date-onomics: How Dating Became a Lopsided Numbers Game* (Workman Publishing, 2015). A former senior writer at *Fortune* and *Money*, Jon was named to AlwaysOn Network's list of "Power Players in Technology Business Media." His work has also appeared in *Barron's*, *Bloomberg Businessweek*, *New York* magazine, *Time*, the *Daily Mail*, the *New York Post*, and the *Washington Post*. Jon is a familiar face and voice on television and radio, having made guest appearances on ABC's *Good Morning America*, BBC World Service, CNBC, CNN, MSNBC, National Public Radio, and Fox News—discussing a wide range of topics from the dating market to the stock market to the oil market. A graduate of Brown University, Jon lives with his family in Larchmont, New York.